CTRL+

HARD

ALT+

RESET

DELETE.

FRAMING DIVERSITY, EQUITY, AND INCLUSION AS THE NEW NORMAL

MARLO RENCHER, PHD, CDE & MARLIN G. WILLIAMS

NOT EVERYTHING THAT
IS FACED CAN BE
CHANGED, BUT NOTHING
CAN BE CHANGED UNTIL IT
IS FACED.

JAMES BALDWIN

TABLE OF CONTENTS

ACKNOWLEDGMENTS

MARLO RENCHER

Writing this book in the middle of a pandemic while processing the death of George Floyd and the weight of all those who preceded and followed him in death was a daunting task. But it was spiritually necessary.

I am deeply grateful to the sister of my heart, Marlin Williams. Our friendship is a jewel that I treasure. I appreciate you lending your experiences, expertise, and stories to this book. I've learned so much from you. I love you and I look forward to sharing what we know with the world.

My husband Charles and daughters Mali and Imani are my foundation. Charles, loving you and being loved by you is such a joy and a privilege. Mali and Imani, your brilliance and beauty clarifies what is most important to me each day. My family's acceptance and encouragement of my ambition and work ethic allows me to be my best. Thank you, my loves.

My mother and father, Robert and Norma Jenkins, my brother, Robert Jenkins, Jr., and the rest of my family have been a steadfast support throughout my life. I love and appreciate you so much for the values, humor, and gratitude you instilled in me.

This book would not have been possible without our writing team village. Thanks to Jill McKellan for your unique perspective and contributions to the text. Thanks to Nichole Christian for your contributions, developmental editing, saintly patience, and passionate enthusiasm for this project. Thanks to Sonya Vann DeLoach for her copyediting. Thanks so much to the fabulous Yolanda Spearman for breathing life into our words in the audio version of this book.

Last, but certainly not least, thanks to all those doing the tough, often underappreciated and definitely underestimated work of diversity, equity, and inclusion. I'm proud to lift you up, to work alongside you, and to learn from you. Thank you for everything you are and everything you give. I love you.

MARLIN WILLIAMS

I've worked in the field of diversity, equity, and inclusion for over 25 years; however, as I was writing this book we were going through a pandemic, the televised re-introduction of systemic racism and the insurrection at the US Capitol. There were days I wanted to stop but continuing this journey was intentional. My voice and this book was the vehicle I needed to speak my truth and share with the world.

My Soror and sister–Marlo Rencher. Your presence has enhanced my life, I feel so blessed that we found each other. Thank you for pushing me to do more and realize my dreams. Without you this book would not be possible. I love you, and I'm so blessed to know you. You can't get rid of me now. I'm here to stay!

My daughter Morgan, my heartbeat. Morgan, I feel so blessed that God chose me to be your mom. When I told you that I was co-writing a book, you didn't doubt me once. We've been through a lot, baby girl, and never once did you give up on me. I adore and love you.

Greg, my amazing husband. I truly believe that our connection was no coincidence. I appreciate your unwavering support. I love you! My mom and dad, Eunice and Walter L. Wilson, Sr., you started me on this journey toward racial equality early in life. Our home was filled with books and conversations about our history. Thank you for being my greatest cheerleaders and for instilling in me the belief that all things are possible. My brother, Walter Wilson, Jr. I adore you sweetheart, you will always be by baby.

Special thanks to my BFF Yolanda Spearman for providing the voice for this book by sharing your voice-over talent. We became high school locker partners more than 30 years ago, and I'm so grateful to still call you my sister and friend.

Audra Bohannon, diversity, equity, and inclusion expert extraordinaire. You are my sister. You taught me to choose to suffer less and that lesson has changed my life. Thank you for mentoring and loving me.

Last but not least, I thank all the civil rights pioneers and those who have lost their lives as they continued the fight. Your tenacity keeps us going and because of you we will not stop.

MARLO RENCHER AND MARLIN WILLIAMS

Both of us want to express our sincere thanks to Leslie Graham Andrews for her feedback and input in the creation of this book.

QUOTES

"We are at a tipping point where our collective
will for progress has exposed and disrupted our
deeply held habits of inequity.

We cannot go back."

MARLO RENCHER

"Inclusion is the essential business imperative today. It
drives new market expansion, innovation, employee retention,
and operational efficiency."

MARLO RENCHER

"Diversity, equity and inclusion work is the ultimate
innovation. It requires you to create a self-perpetuating
culture that helps your team unlock their best, most creative
and most productive selves."

MARLO RENCHER

"If diversity is being invited to the party and inclusion is being asked to the dance, belonging is when the DJ is playing your jam."

MARLIN WILLIAMS

"Data doesn't lie. You've got to take the snapshot to see the change and to make the change. True inclusion demands we look."

MARLIN WILLIAMS

"If organizations don't see the need to course correct during this time of televised and blatant discrimination, perhaps they never will."

MARLIN WILLIAMS

"Inclusion is not just about opening the door. It's about strategically inviting people to bring their whole selves into the culture, into the organization."

MARLIN WILLIAMS

PART ONE

WELCOME TO THE MOMENT

This is our moment. Stop. Read those words again. Slowly.

Take them in because everything that this book was born to challenge and change begins with you, your buy-in, and that of others like you.

A hard true fact sits before all of us. It's time that we, the brave, the bruised and the honest, embrace what we know. We are the people we've been waiting for - the people willing to risk the discomfort of reenvisioning everything in order to reset the ways we work, we live, and ultimately win.

Are you ready?

We already know your answer. You did not open this book by accident. Whether your heart or your job sent you, you're here with good reason. We see you, and we welcome you to the work. Thank you for honoring whatever brought you to the belief that America, and corporate America specifically, is not just having a moment. This is *the* moment.

With a combined seventy-five years of business and entrepreneurial leadership between us, we know with great clarity that we've reached the point of no return. Now or never. Every generation has a movement-making moment, a chance to create lasting change. Those of us who've witnessed missed opportunities, micro and macro workplace mistreatments, we see the horror and also the opportunity to fully acknowledge the racial reckoning before us and prepare to rise from it together.

Diversity, equity and inclusion work is not for the faint of heart. It is not work that everyone can do. We have honed the skills required, so we know that it takes time and practice to develop expertise. Yet we also know from experience the good that can grow when like minds choose collective focus. We must all be willing to look at the vast range of inequity that this moment has brought into stark relief without flinching. As the great author and thinker James Baldwin warned: "Nothing can be changed until it is faced."

This is the choice. Those of us who've patiently cultivated hope for a better future know that we are precisely where we need to be. Our world has the opportunity to accept the restorative power of truth and to experience meaningful change. We did not arrive at this moment by accident. No, we were carried here by an unfortunate yet collective willingness to look away instead of challenging the legacy of unchecked systems, injustice and inequity. The patterns have poisoned our policies for too many decades to count.

We know the truth of these words from years of personal encounters with exclusionary workplace policies and entrenched bias across the corporate and nonprofit sectors. We have witnessed, and at times been victims of, a blatant disregard for the value of diversity and inclusion.

In order to fully realize their potential, these values must not only be articulated, they must be championed. It is mind-blowing that we are well into the twenty-first century and yet we are still experiencing Black firsts in the workplace and in government.

We could spend these pages wailing in frustration and wallowing in a statistical wasteland, continually regurgitating the problem. This is not that kind of book. We choose the tough, rigorous, and rewarding path of problem-solving. Our sights are set on a new mutual opportunity to reset everything from head to heart through an active approach to diversity, equity, and inclusion. By *active* we mean fully engaged and committed, across our various divides, to the work of bringing just, fair and equitable strategies and conversations into every corner of the business world from the factory floor to the C suite table.

In the midst of a 2020s global pandemic and the rise of racial reckoning, we watched the world pause. From our various quarantines, lockdown places, and vantage points, we rediscovered, and in some cases uncovered, the meaning of essential and nonessential work.

The privileged learned to be grateful for an underpaid and underappreciated workforce and to underpaid front-line workers. The critical work of those who kept the nation's supply of food and basic services from sudden collapse for us all has been made plain. The service and health industries' willingness to welcome educational, lifestyle, racial, gender, and sexual differences of all kinds was crucial at a time when the world literally came to a stop.

The devastating wreckage of this pandemic took a personal and professional toll on all of us. It gave each of us an opportunity for self-reflection and change. As diversity and inclusion professionals, we saw a new purpose for our lives. It's no longer enough to wish for the reset that we know to be possible from our deep experience in the corporate, tech and nonprofit worlds. It's time to do the hard work, and to use our years to help lead the way for corporate leaders who truly want the benefits of more just and inclusive business environments.

The moment is ours to transform. We will change it by shifting our calibration of what is acceptable to tolerate and moving past comfort to act. We will change it by training ourselves to perceive a world with more just possibilities. We must vigorously resist that which does not fall within these new standards.

Embracing inclusion and equity is not an act of weakness or surrender. It's a business imperative rooted in common sense. Strategic fairness profits all. It helps smart companies build a pipeline of talent with powerful ideas and unique perspectives. It empowers the voices and views of the wide range of generations in the workplace. A culture that inspires belonging in all of its team members has a clear advantage in the fight for talent.

In this long moment of rebuilding, the only way to lose is to continue looking away instead of running toward the just and attainable doable changes right in front of us. And there are many. We'll write a brighter future only if we're finally ready to train ourselves to look, listen, and learn from what we hear, no matter how uncomfortable it may seem at first.

We are, after all, in this moment—the pain and the possibility—together.

Let's Reset the future right. Now.

CHAPTER ONE

ON BELONGING

MARLO'S STORY.

The first time I felt like I truly didn't belong at my workplace was during a summer internship at an automotive plant just outside Detroit. It was, I believe, my second internship. My first internship was working in private banking at a large regional bank headquartered in the city. At the bank, I was developing strategies for marketing services to wealthy customers in a posh office overlooking the Detroit River.

I was born on the west side of Detroit to a firmly middle class family of teachers. While being wealthy wasn't a completely alien concept, it always felt aspirational and just out of reach. But I knew I could fit in as someone who could be paid fairly well marketing to rich folks, so that was all right. I enjoyed the work. I was fairly good at it. My supervisor and the other workers in the department were White, but we were located in the heart of a majority Black city, my home. It was different from the jobs at the retail stores and movie theater that I'd had before–a little less fun, a lot more pay.

Interning at the plant was another experience entirely. It was a summer later in my undergraduate years. I worked for the assistant plant manager, a hard-driving White woman who had made her bones in a less than welcoming atmosphere for female managers. It was the early 1990s, and there was a low level of normalized, casual misogyny and racism that was to be expected in such places. Jokes and offhand comments that would not be acceptable in the workplace now were commonplace. During that time, in most white collar workplaces being anything aside from a straight White male meant being the *other*.

I had been brought into a management position, albeit a junior one, and was therefore expected to socialize with managers. The management team was relatively small in number, exclusively White, predominantly male, pre-sumably straight, and definitely older. The line workers at the automotive plant whose shift coincided with my work hours were primarily Black and ranged in age from just out of high school to beyond retirement age. Reinforcing the racial lines of demarcation between these two groups was a clear cultural separation. Line workers existed in their own world, complete with its own hierarchies and rules of engagement. The physical layout of the factory floor centers production, not the individual. It is clear when you are working in the factory that you are part of a much greater whole. You are replaceable, but you are also part of a distinct community designed for a specific, shared purpose. So I felt a greater sense of a specific, shared existence when on the factory floor. Line workers even had their own internal, non-sanctioned lottery operation.

The lives of managers seemed to be more reflective of the outside world. Their experience was bureaucratic but more individually centered than factory life. They were located in bright air-conditioned offices and their movements were less regimented. Their daily activities were dealing with administrative needs of the factory and managing the output of the line workers.

Like many Detroiters, especially Black ones, my personal history was more tied to the line than to the managerial desk. My grandfather worked for 40 years in a Ford factory. He also ran numbers. For the uninitiated, this means he was a part of the internal lottery system at the plant. During my time working at the plant, I related more to the folks on the factory floor than to the people I was supposed to be working most closely with, the managers. The plant was also located in a White enclave outside the city of Detroit that was not overly friendly to outsiders. Most managers lived nearby and connected with each other outside of work. It took me about 45 minutes each day to get to the plant. I rose early each morning to make it to my desk by 7:30 am. I remember the one time early in my internship that my boss called me to the managers' lunch table to eat.

Both managers and line workers ate in a huge cafeteria, but self-segregation was the norm. I was introduced to the men at the managers' table, and I said my hellos. After a somewhat awkward series of introductions, the previous conversation resumed. I felt quite a few eyes on me from the factory workers. I was an anomaly--a young Black woman seated with the older, White male bosses. Aside from the first hello, none of the bosses initiated any interaction with me during that lunch. It was uncomfortable and I ended up eating by myself at my desk most days. Although most of my daily interactions were with the managers, the kinship I felt with the factory workers remained stronger. A few months later, right before I completed my internship, a Black factory worker I didn't know came up to me and told me she was proud of me

I felt that kinship returned to me in several other small acknowledgments, a nod here or a word there. I never felt that connection with the managers or my supervisor. At my end of internship review, my supervisor noted that I was too sleepy in the morning and that I didn't do enough to interact with the other managers. It never did feel right to me to be just a summer intern, and yet one of the highest ranking Black people at the plant. I never shared my struggle with belonging with my boss. I didn't get the sense that she would empathize or even understand what I was feeling. She had been able to operate in this environment where women managers were few and far between. She was doing just fine. That internship was my first experience with feeling that I did not belong at work. It taught me that a critical part of being a good leader is to create a context for commonality with teams. People may find it easier to relate to others because they share the same race or gender. For others, it may be easier to connect to their peers because they went to the same college, or because they went to college. While finding these commonalities, we must also recognize where people can feel excluded. As teams diversify, they need to be actively managed with an inclusion lens because the barriers to belonging can be higher.

As authors of this book and professionals with related expertise, Marlin Williams and I understand the importance of inclusion in the workplace. As Generation X Black women, we have each endured its absence in some of our work experiences. Inclusion is distinct from diversity, yet diversity is required for inclusion. Without diversity, belonging is passive, a condition acquired by birth or shared background. The presence of difference and diversity transforms inclusion to something active that must overcome our human inclination to favor the safety of our tribes. In uncertain times, such as those ushered in by 2020's COVID-19 pandemic and the inflection point catalyzed by George Floyd's murder, it is natural for people to crave safety, especially the safety found in familiar people, places, and things. Yet we know in our hearts that the past holds no safety for any of us, since it brought us here. We must move forward into transformation, into something new.

WHY RESET NOW

Workplaces around the world, from mom-and-pop establishments to global enterprises are facing a hard reset on their relationships with their employees. Two major forces–the COVID-19 pandemic and a wider awakening to the negative and pervasive impact of racism and anti-Blackness–have rewritten the rules of engagement and exposed the dysfunction across organizational cultures.

All team members are valuable, from those on the front line whose needs have been ignored to the isolated middle managers who are ostracized from their peers for having the perceived wrong background, gender, or sexual orientation. Those who live at the intersection of outsider groups are especially vulnerable to feeling excluded. Many companies have not prioritized developing environments that embrace all of their team members.

COVID-19 highlighted the stark reality is that our world needs everyone's value to be recognized, yet it is often the case that those who are supported, respected, and paid the least are the most essential to its day-to-day functioning.

DEVELOPING SENSITIVITY TO THE STRUGGLE

In an article written by Rev. Dr. William J. Barber II, co-founder of the nonprofit Repairers of the Breach and co-chair of the Poor People's Campaign, and then-Rep. Joe Kennedy III1, (D-MA), they shared that the COVID-19 pandemic has forced low-wage workers without the liberty or luxury of being able to stay home to put their lives on the line for the rest of us who do. They go on to state that all workers have the right to five essentials in their lives: food security, housing security, healthcare, living wages, and clean air and water (Barber II & Kennedy III, 2020). Dr. Barber shared valuable insight when he said, "Pandemics spread and exploit the fissures of society. And the United States has many, many wounds, open wounds from our structural racism, and the criminalization of poverty, and the refusal to address poverty. And those realities made us even more susceptible to the pandemic." (Capehart, 2020).

For many who already have access to these essentials, it may be easy to forget that there are millions who do not. Some of those millions are your coworkers. You may have even experienced insecurity in one of these areas yourself. Arming yourself with a heightened awareness of the data concerning these essentials is critical to decentering your experience and understanding the struggles that some of your team members may be experiencing.

According to the United States Department of Agriculture, more than 35 million people struggle with hunger in the United States, including more than 11 million children (Coleman-Jensen et al., 2020, pp. 1–3). As of August 2020, it is estimated that more than 50 million people, including 17 million children, may experience food insecurity in 2020 (Feeding America, 2020). The pandemic has also exacerbated the problem of homelessness. According to the Department for Housing and Urban Development (HUD), on any given night in January 2019, 560,715 people were homeless.

Nearly two-thirds of those counted lived in shelters. About a quarter of them were deemed "chronically homeless," which, by the definition HUD adopted in 2015, meant that they had been "living in a place not meant for human habitation, a safe haven, or in an emergency shelter" for 12 months running or for that total over a three-year stretch. As of July 2020, as many as 23 million renters faced eviction. The second quarter of 2020's estimated US gross domestic product experienced the worst economic contraction (-32.9 percent) since the Bureau of Economic Analysis started releasing its advance estimates in 1947, which, coupled with record-setting unemployment claims paints a dim future for food and housing stability for a significant portion of US families.

Before COVID-19, health disparities between Black, Latinx, and White people were widespread, significant, and well-documented. With the onset of the pandemic, the rates of infection and mortality in Black and Latinx communities have been consistently higher than for White communities due to pre-existing health and economic disparities. According to the Centers for Disease Control and Prevention, death rates among Black people fifty-five to sixty-four years old are higher than for White people aged sixty-five to seventy-four, and death rates are higher for Blacks aged sixty-five to seventy-four than for Whites aged seventy-five to eighty-four, and so on. In every age category, Black people are dying from COVID at roughly the same rate as White people more than a decade older. Age-specific death rates for Hispanic/Latino people fall in between. These disparities can be observed at all ages, but are especially marked in somewhat younger age groups. These disparities can be seen more clearly by comparing the ratio of death rates among Black and His-panic/Latino people to the rate for White people in each age category. Among those aged forty-five to fifty-four, for example, Black and Hispanic/Latino death rates are at least six times higher than for Whites.

As a result of the higher mortality rate for Black and Latinx communities, more individuals are impacted. More of your Black and Latinx colleagues have friends and family who have gotten sick and died from COVID. There is unspo-ken grief carried by some of your team members while keeping a smile on their faces during Zoom calls or while donning a mask and engaging with customers. Combine this stress with processing the trauma of the killings of George Floyd, Breonna Taylor and others and you start to glimpse the painful reality that some of your colleagues might be facing. It may also help you to process your own journey through these crises.

Some of your colleagues, especially those saddled with crushing student loan debt, or those with unemployed or underemployed spouses or partners, are working multiple jobs to make ends meet. Some are struggling to homeschool their children or care for elderly parents. Some even lack clean air and water. It is critical for everyone to open their eyes and see the inequity that these crises have revealed. Without fundamental change, these struggles will become more acute, and push us further apart. We are certain about the need to adapt to the crisis presented to us; we simply need a viable roadmap for us to follow as we create a new normal.

A HIGHER STANDARD OF NORMAL

The new normal in business is to have an environment where companies invest in creating truly inclusive environments. What we mean by an inclusive environment is one where companies nurture their cultures to ensure that all team members are supported, respected, and valued as their authentic selves. Casual dress codes and scattering foosball tables and Nerf guns in break areas represented the first efforts for companies to nurture a culture that included younger team members. Play is a good context for us to tap into our common humanity. Yet there is a great deal more that we can do that considers everyone, from the software engineer to the janitor, from the grocery store bagger to the CEO.

The opportunity of inclusion is that it can become a competitive advantage that enables everyone in an organization to operate as their best self. Diversity and inclusion consulting firm Pope Consulting trademarked a phrase that captures the importance of going beyond diversity to inclusion: Diversity without inclusion is like revenue without profits⸮. The reality is that inclusion is one of the few dimensions of competitive advantage that has not been thoroughly explored and effectively optimized as a management skill. The impact of the pandemic and new level of awareness of racism on inclusion cannot be overstated. This book is filled with solid information to help you to navigate a new framework for inclusion.

You'll contemplate the following questions.

- What are the long-term benefits of treating an authentically inclusive culture as a corporate asset, like brand equity?

- How could we have employees across the organization feel supported, respected, and valued at scale?

- Is there any cap on the benefits that exist when an employee feels valued?

- Are we fundamentally and systemically unable to produce an inclusive culture? What does our history and our data say about this?

- If we cannot create an inclusive culture, what alternative strategies should we consider to remain competitive?

Answers to these pressing questions are the gateway to a stronger future for any business that takes the work and the journey to change seriously.

THE OPPORTUNITY

Diversity and inclusion are not yet topics that are widely taught to young professionals as they move into the working world, at least not in a way that goes beyond performative notions of inclusion. Actual steps on how to create a thriving, inclusive environment still elude the managerial education of most CEOs and high-level executives. And in a world where leaders are managing many competing priorities, how do you gain an audience with someone who wants to talk about the necessary changes that will make inclusion the standard, not the stand-out exception?

There are a few important priorities that should guide your diversity and inclusion strategy development.

- Developing strong leaders who realize the importance of diversity and inclusion

- Understanding the link between inclusion and innovation

- Recruiting and supporting a diverse set of board directors to provide organizational governance

- Adopting a full cycle diversity and inclusion strategy that encompasses all career phases, including recruitment, career development, and succession planning

- Seeing the value and opportunity that exists within each position, from front line positions to the C-suite

We are excited to participate in this transition to a more equitable and exciting workforce that is prepared to handle a future that has inclusion as a driving force.

We are going to show you how to use inclusion to teach those in leadership positions how to continuously innovate to increase diversity and promote inclusion. This is the starting point to taking actions strong enough to make people feel supported, valued, and respected within their workplace.

But before we dive in further, take a trip with us into a scenario that we believe illustrates the urgency and the possibility for change inherent in this moment.

Meet Kelly. She is a thirty-something White millennial woman who has been newly hired as the chief diversity officer for ABC Corp., a manufacturing firm based in the Midwest that employs about 700 people. She's excited about her new role and responsibilities. She's also a little anxious because it is her first real opportunity to do diversity and inclusion work as a formal part of her job description.

In her first few weeks at ABC, her first priority is to get a clear picture of who is employed at the organization. She analyzes internal human resource data, which describes the patterns of gender, age, race, and ethnicity of ABC Corp. employees. She goes deeper and analyzes the relative pay, managerial attainment, and rate of promotion within the company. The results are immediately concerning. There are clear and glaring disparities in the way people are being treated based on their backgrounds. Kelly's first step to address these inequities is to go beyond the data to the people, so she begins to speak with team members across the organization to gather their perspectives.

The more Kelly learns, the greater her concerns become. Based on her conversations, the front line manufacturing workers feel as if the company is not adequately respecting or compensating them. In addition, ABC's Black and Brown workers are severely overrepresented on the front lines, and severely underrepresented in the ranks of management and they are painfully aware of that fact.

As a result of this dynamic, there is an uneasy relationship between workers. There was a palpable sense of "Us" and "Them" that predated the racial reckoning brought about by George Floyd's murder in 2020. However, that incident gave ABC Corp. workers of all races, genders, and backgrounds a new sense of freedom to speak out about their conditions rather than to accept them without comment. Those conversations were happening on internal Slack channels and external Facebook and Instagram groups.

Kelly feels a sense of urgency about presenting her findings to senior leadership. However, she is hesitant about making recommendations for change because the issues she has identified are systemic and widespread. Kelly simply does not have the tools to address this sort of problem.

Knowing that immediate and massive action is required, Kelly arranges a meeting with ABC Corp.'s senior leadership. She begins to express the findings she has unraveled. As she looks at each of them, the leadership team glances at each other and then, with a collective sense of resignation mingled with a touch of defensiveness, they look back to her. Kelly realizes that the news she has delivered is not new.

A conversation begins. As it turns out, these company leaders live in constant fear that the problems within the company will be publicly exposed. ABC Corp. is one viral video away from a significant negative impact on their economic health, the positive brand they've nurtured through investment, and the stable reputation they've earned through fifty years of consistent performance.

About half of the leadership team is resentful about this hazard. They believe that ABC Corp. pays good wages to its employees and offers great opportunities for those who put in the work. They don't feel obligated to offer more than what they already do–a good job with benefits and a paycheck. The other half are more sensitive to the monochromatic nature of their middle level and senior management teams, and to the opposing optics on ABC's front line. The pandemic and protests opened their eyes to the everyday racism that they had always understood to be just the way things were. They believe that a fundamental change is overdue.

Everyone believes that Kelly's preliminary findings could be just the tip of the iceberg of ABC's troubles. They want to lead a company with a positive culture and team members that are proud to work there. The more prosperous companies that ABC Corp. competes against seem to reflect a strong sense of community among their workers. As a group, the senior leadership team resolves to support Kelly as she creates a path forward. Her mandate is to create and implement a plan that would heal and strengthen the relationship that ABC Corp. has with all of its employees, resulting in a better company with better overall results.

Where does Kelly, do any of us, begin?

CHAPTER TWO

ON UNCOMFORTABLE TRUTHS

On May 25, 2020, Amy Cooper, a White woman, was walking her dog in New York City's Central Park. She let the dog run without a leash in the Ramble area of the park, a place where leashes are required.

Christian Cooper, a Black man unrelated to Ms. Cooper, was bird watching in the Ramble. He asked Amy Cooper to leash her dog, and she refused. He offered the dog a treat. Amy Cooper yelled "Don't you touch my dog!" and placed a call to 911. Christian Cooper started recording the encounter. The recording begins with Amy Cooper approaching Christian and pointing her finger in his face. He says, "Please don't come close to me." She said to

Christian, "I'm calling the cops... I'm gonna tell them there's an African-American man threatening my life." She pulled out her phone and began calling the police. She told the operator that "There is an African-American man—I'm in Central Park—he is recording me and threatening myself and my dog. Please send the cops immediately!" The video ends with Christian telling her "thank you" when she leashes her dog. When the police arrived, both Christian and Amy were gone.

Amy Cooper made a real threat to Christian Cooper's life when she led her complaint to the police with Christian's race and gender. The history of police killings of Black people of both genders is tragic. The fact that Amy Cooper intentionally weaponized her race and gender to intensify the bias against Christian could have easily led to another tragic result.

The fact that Christian Cooper is a Harvard graduate, a senior biomedical editor at an established publication, and a groundbreaking writer and editor for Marvel Comics shouldn't matter, but it does. His accomplishments make it easy to see the assumptions and racism that fueled Amy Cooper's actions. But the threat to Christian's life is inexcusable, whether he graduated from Harvard or he was the proud holder of a GED. Acceptability under the White gaze should not be what grants Black people the right to be safe from threat. It is basic humanity that should provide that pass. For every Christian Cooper who inspires a collective national outrage, there are many more, less accomplished people who endure the indignities of systemic racism and casual White nationalism.

As diversity, equity, and inclusion professionals, we are no strangers to that dynamic. We had the opportunity to hear a story about how that example plays out in real life. We were conducting a cultural audit where team members were invited to share their stories and perspectives. One young man talked about his life. He has worked on the factory floor for a very long time. And he is good at his craft. At this meeting, he began to talk to us about his experiences in America as a Black man. He had been targeted, like many have, and pulled over while driving. He was held in handcuffs simply because he fit a particular description. Another time, he was leaving a restaurant with his friends and their clothes fit the general description of a man wanted for a crime that had been committed a few blocks away. The police held them at gunpoint. He was terrified and knew he had to respond in a way that did not get him killed. He'd just been getting something to eat with friends but he was being profiled. The story could have ended tragically. The tragedy would have been compounded by the fact that no one filmed the encounter. It would have been an incident framed by the police report and the officers' narratives. It is highly unlikely that the man's death would have resulted in charges being brought against the officers for killing an innocent man. The uncomfortable truth is that these encounters happen all too frequently. The deeper truth is that the racism that underlies these events informs many other, less physically dangerous incidents faced by people of color, and specifically Black people.

The man who was stopped was a frontline worker. He also happened to have a bachelor's degree. He had done the work and had the focus that the accomplishment requires. But his worth should not be tied to his accomplishment. The degree is not what should make us say that the profiling was wrong. For that to be true, it implies that Black people must accomplish something to be worthy to be treated with care and consideration.

Now it is clear that the man was profiled by the police, but he is also being profiled in another way. The company he works for is an exciting one, with a bright future. The young man knew that and took a job as a frontline worker to get his foot in the door. He didn't have any relationships with any current workers that could make it easier for him to get a job that correlates more closely with his degree. We found through discussions with white collar employees that they do not perceive frontline workers as being a potential talent pool for higher potential jobs with higher pay at the company. Despite the fact that they have frontline workers with intelligence, skill, and even graduate-level degrees, it did not occur to company executives to tap into this talent. So the oft-lamented pipeline problem that is typically raised in response to dismal rates of diversity within a company has the potential to be solved by a change in perception.

The change in perception required is not simple, because it is perception that is deeply embedded in American culture. The idea that the majority of people of color, and particularly Black people, should be a permanent underclass is an uncomfortable truth since America's founding. This consistent condition of Black life is rarely explicitly stated, but informs many of our interactions. The Black Lives Matter movement is revolutionary in that its premise–that Black Lives Matter on their face, regardless of the respectability of a Black person's accomplishments or the fungibility of their talents–flies in the face of the default devaluation of Black people that justifies our living with so many everyday inequities. There are so many things that all of us, Black, White, everyone, take as the normal state of Black life, from living with polluted food, air, and water to utterly broken educational systems to high infant and maternal-mortality rates. The persistent gap in capital access and household wealth are staggering monuments to racial inequity that we have all gotten used to. These Grand Canyons of inequities require the same amount of focus and attention that the real Grand Canyon requires to truly appreciate their scope and depth.

A radical approach to corporate innovation is to recognize this perception and to change it through inclusion. What makes this approach radical and innovative is that treating all team members as full humans with unlimited potential could unlock much more value for the company where they work than by assessing value through the limited perception that has been the rule. So how can we get there? That's part of what this book is about. But first, we will explore how the COVID-19 pandemic has opened our eyes to the need for change.

COVID-19: A CALL FOR CHANGE

The COVID-19 crisis has unmasked a lot in terms of workplace inequity. The crisis dramatically highlighted how dependent we are on people who are working at minimum wage rates and probably in marginalized jobs.

This laid bare the difference between people who are secure in their jobs and those who are not. A worker in manufacturing who works on the factory floor does not have the luxury to be able to work from home. Cars still need to be assembled, clothing produced, and other goods made. How do we make these people feel valued and respected, while others are sitting at home, safely?

In a Slate article by Dahlia Lithwick, she talked about how we may be doing a disservice to our essential workers by calling them heroes. No matter how many honks of support and words of kindness we express to them, it does zero to change the policies, either governmental or in business, that create a dangerous pathway for them . Yes, we admire and respect them. However, treating them like martyrs will not solve the problem. More is deserved, and more is possible.

We talk about voting out what doesn't promote the change we need. This is a solution, for certain, and it spotlights what happened in Wisconsin's April 2019 primary, where people stood in line for hours just to have the opportunity to vote six feet apart. And masks on, they heroically endured it. However, Mark Joseph Stern, a colleague of Lithwick's described it well when he wrote: "We should be inspired by Wisconsinite's refusal to let Republicans silence their voices. But we should also be horrified that some Americans may have literally sacrificed their lives to exercise this constitutional right." (Lithwick, 2020).

This is not about Republican versus Democrat; it's about a failed system that has not done what it should to protect the constitutional rights of all. And make no mistake about it, we are all in this together. How work is done in the future will impact every person in some way.

We all rely on somebody along the line. The delivery driver, the grocery store clerk, the people who make our cars, and endless other things we deem essential. These people do more than make something we need; they have something beyond the obvious to offer at their job level, or where they desire to advance.

Others face a different situation. Working from home has become a new normal for them, but one fraught with challenges. They were never prepared to have their lives at home be exposed to their team members. They may have housing insecurity or other challenges with their homes, problems with child or elder care that disrupt their meetings, lack of access to reliable internet that negatively impacts how they are represented on screen, or a toxic or abusive home situation that can spill over into work interactions.

Companies that recognize and mitigate these dynamics will reap significant rewards in increased productivity and employee retention.

One initiative for change came from Michigan, where Governor Gretchen Whitmer set up a coronavirus racial disparity task force. The official purpose was to find out why the novel coronavirus disproportionately affected Michigan's African-American community.

When asked about this, Whitmer stated, "While African Americans represent 13.6 percent of our state's population, they represent a staggering 40 percent of the deaths from COVID-19." The task force's goal is to investigate and study strategies to address the disparity in these numbers. In addition, it will look into the systematic inequalities pertaining to race that have amplified the death rate in the state's Black community (O'Reilly, 2020).

It should be noted that Whitmer was not the first person to notice this disparity.

Civil rights leader Rev. Jesse Jackson also said: "It's America's unfinished business—we're free, but not equal. There's a reality check that has been brought by the coronavirus, that exposes the weakness and the opportunity." (Cutter & Maloney, 2020).

The pervasive combination of bias, privilege, fragility, a lack of empathy, blind spots, and system inertia make diversity and inclusion difficult for an organization. By exposing what these terms imply, we can lay out the problems that are prevalent in the workplace. Especially with the way we now have to operate in order to better manage the fallout from COVID-19.

BIAS REVEALED

All people have biases based on their backgrounds and their unique life perspectives.

People tend to feel more comfortable with people who they perceive as having the same background. As a result, hiring patterns often match that comfort level. The result can be a group of people working together who are more of an echo chamber. This equates to fewer challenges to a particular mindset. The idea of bringing in people who have a different mindset or array of experiences is not considered.

These differences come in many forms. It could be the school that you attended. Some companies prefer to recruit from a specific school and do things a particular way. Therefore, continuously hiring these people creates a culture where things are continuously done the same way and the challenge of new ideas is lacking. Ideas that challenge the status quo can make a company grow stronger. New voices are needed, but with insular company cultures, the few that may exist can be drowned out.

Did you know that you need at least three different people to voice a new perspective for it typically to be considered?

Openly acknowledging that it takes a collective of personalities, backgrounds, and experiences to ensure a well-rounded organization is what is required. There is strength in diversity. See Appendix A for a detailed list of the terms that fit with ways bias are expressed.

We often speak about how diversity adds to a company, but we are also people who have used our diverse backgrounds to add to our companies. We know the positive impact to performance and culture that different perspectives bring because we've been the ones that have made a difference in our organizations. We've seen others who have been a culture add, rather than merely a culture fit.

MARLIN'S HARD RESET

It's no accident that we chose *Hard Reset* as the title of the book you're holding. Both of us know the value of hard resets because we've each lived through and grown from a few of them.

Though she has an impressive track record, wealth of knowledge and executive-level experience helping companies think smarter about diversity, equity and inclusion, Marlin's life was set for an entirely different and somewhat unlikely path.

She was on her way to becoming a mortician. The choice seemed sure and solid. "I was working at two funeral homes in Detroit. Then a classmate told me about a program through the Compuware Corporation where, if you had a college degree, they would teach you to program in seven languages in 13 weeks."

Marlin's curiosity in that moment and her willingness to explore the possibilities of change literally reset her entire life. "I didn't know what programming was. But it offered more money than I was making at the funeral home. So I just jumped in and committed to learning how to do it. It was one of the best—and hardest—experiences of my life. I considered quitting almost every day because my programs just wouldn't work, but I kept going back." Coding soon catapulted Marlin to heights she barely had time to dream about.

Marlin helped to open the doors for others at Compuware, ultimately becoming its global chief diversity officer. She helped to ease the large corporation's move from the suburbs to downtown Detroit, helping to catalyze the renaissance that is in evidence today. She later served as deputy CIO for the city of Detroit, playing a key role in the city's successful hosting of Super Bowl XL. She later started and grew a technology staffing firm to over a million dollars in revenue. Ultimately the business failed, and she had to reinvent herself again.

"I was at the height of my career. I had the most beautiful home. My daughter was in a private school… It was like a fairytale. Then, life knocked me not on my knees, but on my back. I remember waking up every day not knowing what to do. But then I remembered something my father told me; he said, 'Everything you ever need … you have it inside of you. You've just forgotten that.'"

Leaning into her father's wisdom, Marlin, who was suddenly unemployed and divorced, summoned the courage to choose change once again. She let her passion for people—particularly women and people of color—and problem solving lead her back to the front lines of opportunity. "I was on a panel called 'Education 2.0 for Americans 2.0.' At the end of the session, they said, "What are you going to do to bridge the gender gap in tech?"

Marlin soon answered the question by creating Sisters Code, an organization designed to empower women ages 25 to 85 by providing them the tools they need to re-career into technology fields. Today, Sisters Code supports over 3,000 women on their tech career journey.

To this day, Marlin still looks to the lessons of her big life pivot in everything that she does. "Change happens from an intentional decision and intentional action. You can't just hope your way into personal or system change," she says. "You have to put the work in, analyze the problem, and then apply your best thinking, your biggest dream, and an open mind. This isn't something I've read about. It's my life."

NAVIGATING UNFAMILIAR SPACES

We have had first hand encounters with navigating change and new environments. Marlo used to be a vice president at a university. The university was in a politically conservative, majority-White county and she was employed there during the time Trump was president.

During Marlo's tenure at the university, she thought a lot about race.

"I'm convinced that the subject pervaded my thoughts more thoroughly than my colleagues, just about all of whom were White. The town had once been home to an active grand wizard of the Ku Klux Klan and had maintained a reputation as a 'sundown town', a place where it was unsafe for people of color, and Black people in particular, to be after the sun went down."

When I started the position, I had the kinds of concerns that I was sure none of my colleagues had. What if I got pulled over? This was a city where I feared that getting pulled over would not end with a simple ticket. The tragedy of Sandra Bland's 2015 death in Texas was still fresh, and it shadowed my commute. I was concerned with promoting the university to Black students without being absolutely sure of their safety.

When I first came to work at the university, I taught courses and got to know the students, most of whom had grown up in the area. As my responsibilities increased, I joined the university's cabinet, attended board of trustee meetings, and served on regional economic development boards. As a result, I got to know many well-to-do local businesspeople. I had my own biases about the kind of people who live in sundown towns. As is often the case, my individual experiences with people were different from what I thought they would be. We each had our biases, those never left, but we were able to cultivate good relationships. I had many opportunities to share perspectives and ideas with the people I met. The different perspectives made the experience enriching. We were able to move our interactions beyond our biases. The biases never left, but they became more informed through individual connection."

COMFORTABLE LIES

The idea that life provides everyone with the same opportunities for financial security, health, and overall happiness is a comfortable *lie*. Privilege is power. It is power that affords some groups better access to resources than others. While that is an inherently unfair situation, what makes privilege so complicated is that it confers power in a way that makes that power seem earned or invisible.

For example, the gaps in health, wealth, educational, and other quality of life resources between heterosexual White men and others in society have been clear and persistent for a long time. It has been the case for so long that the gaps become invisible. That is, White men may assume that either everyone lives the way they do, or they may not ever think about those who do not. Another dynamic that keeps the status quo is that people who do not have access to the same level of resources may also not think about a future where they can have access. That future is either crushed by the inexorable weight of what has always been, or it is something that may seem to take too much precious energy to fight for, with no guarantee of success.

The rewards of privilege can also feel like something earned. Imagine a college classroom with a young African-American woman brought up in a two-parent, highly educated, upper-middle-class household. She may have a distinct advantage in completing her degree successfully over a middle-aged White man who is returning to school as a nontraditional student to try to become the first in his family to complete college. She may earn a higher GPA than he does, but he needed to overcome more to get to the same result.

The power that comes from privilege comes with blind spots. These blind spots enable the comfortable lie that the resources accumulated from privilege are earned or available to all. One of the effects of COVID-19 is that it exposed our shared system of blind spots. It became impossible to ignore the differences in the way people are treated.

According to an article in *The Atlantic* written by Adam Serwer, philosopher Charles Mills described a racial contract as "the implicit agreement among members of a society to follow the rules." It is a part of our societal contract. He gives examples, which include acting lawfully and contesting agreed-upon rules by nonviolent means.

Challenges arise when the rules present themselves differently to different races and cultures. Its context becomes skewed because certain groups see differences in how what is right and what is wrong are managed. Examples of this include:

- Police officers are typically not prosecuted in the same way if they kill a person of color as they would be for killing someone White

- A different set of rules for behavior and expected productivity exists for a person of color in the workplace

- The health and well-being of those in the lower-income levels (often people of color) are not as important as those of financial affluency

Whether intentionally or unintentionally supporting this ingrained behavior, the consequences create disparity between races, their actions, and the consequences or results of them. Mills also stated, "The terms of the racial contract mean that non-White sub personhood is enshrined simultaneous with White personhood." (Serwer, 2020)

It should be noted that this contract is not a partisan agreement. People across a wide array of the political spectrum see value in its presence. The catch is that it works best for them when it is invisible. But there are times when the contract's inequality is exposed. George Floyd's murder by a White officer in Minneapolis was one of those explosive moments. When the inequity of the contract is exposed, we are forced to choose whether or not we are okay with its flaws. A situation was once relegated to being protested by those in the minority who were being actively oppressed, and silently and passively accepted by those who could afford injustice now demanded allegiance to one side or another.

The shift from living with a comfortable lie to acknowledging an uncomfortable truth requires each of us to take a measure of ourselves. What do we stand for? When do we fight? What do we value? Who are we if we do not make our values known? What do we believe? Are we who we thought we would be in this moment of truth?

ARE YOU RACIST?

If you were to pose this simple question to most White people, "Are you racist?", the answer would most assuredly be "No." Their definition of racism is likely "someone who holds a conscious dislike of people of another race." In this case, they would be correct.

We believe that this matter should be looked at through the lens of *White fragility,* a term coined by Robin Di Angelo, a sociologist who specializes in mapping patterns, and is the author of *The New York Times* bestseller, *White Fragility: Why It's So Hard for White People to Talk About Racism.* The book explores the reflexive defensive tendencies of Whites around conversations about race. White fragility is defined as the disbelieving defensiveness that White people exhibit when their ideas about race and racism are challenged—and particularly when they feel implicated in White supremacy. The concept highlights just how well society is set up to insulate White people from having the uncomfortable conversations that are associated with race and racism. Thinking and feeling like you are not racist is not enough. Di Angelo states:

"Like waves on sand, their patterns form predictable patterns: they will insist that they 'were taught to treat everyone the same,' that they are 'color-bind,' that they don't care if you are pink, purple, or polka-dotted."

(WALDMAN, 2018).

So, whether intentional or not, White fragility holds racism in its place. This results in good-intentioned individuals not really taking steps to remove racist systems because doing so subjects them to an unacceptable level of discomfort.

We may not be able to eliminate White fragility. We hope to work with people to create solutions that incorporate a community's dynamics into the corporate structure. We challenge White people to isolate their feelings of discomfort and simply acknowledge the feeling without making it mean anything. Do not associate the feeling with any value judgments about yourself, about the situation, or about what should be done about the situation. Those judgments can make you feel attacked instead of just uncomfortable. They make you feel the need to reflexively defend yourself rather than deal with the real issues. Just allow the discomfort to exist without connecting it to anything else. Allow the discomfort to simply be information about how you are feeling and nothing else.

THE FRICTION POINTS WITHIN ORGANIZATIONS

Another uncomfortable truth to acknowledge is that organizations are often systemically ill-equipped to be inclusive. There are too many inherent points of friction that stymie implementation. To better understand how friction works within an organization, it pays to understand the concept of inertia. *Inside Energy* reporter Leigh Paterson described inertia as:

"...one of the most basic concepts of physics. Essentially, things that are moving will keep moving unless a force, like friction, causes them to stop. And things that are not moving will continue to not move unless a force, like a gust of wind, causes them to move"

(WIRFS-BROCK & PATERSON, 2017).

Newton's first law of physics is about this. This simple-sounding definition isn't always easy to see. According to Anat Burger, a professor of physics, a better way to understand this is:

"The reason why the concept of inertia was not immediately obvious to everyone before Newton is because our world is filled with sources of friction that act to resist motion. For example, if you give a box a push, it will not continue moving at a constant speed, it will very quickly come to a stop. That is because of the friction acting between the box and the floor. In order to see inertia at work, we need systems that have very low friction, such as in outer space."

(IBID).

Now take this understanding of friction and inertia and apply it to business. As in physics, there are many sources of unseen friction that act on new initiatives. In order for anything new to be implemented, care must be taken to identify the sources of friction and remove or mitigate them. This especially includes any unseen friction.

Policies created to produce more equitable, inclusive workplaces will also encounter friction. It takes rigorous data collection and analysis to identify friction points. For example, identifying and understanding gaps in mobility between people based on gender, ethnicity, and other demographic identifiers can help to highlight and quantify friction.

Dynamics like White fragility make it more important to make these points visible and measurable. If the default response to being shown systemic racial inequities is to shut down and look away from the problem, then it is important to make the problem as "real" as possible. In American culture, the reality of a thing is enhanced by its ability to be quantifiably measured.

Points of friction only become obvious to people who do not want to see them when the forces acting to stop progress are exposed, measured, and made plain. For example, efforts to have a more inclusive workforce may encounter friction, resulting in leadership that is 100 percent White in a community where White people are 55 percent of the population. When you break down sources of friction, such as the hiring team choosing to recruit from warm referrals from current employees, or not employing a specialist to help diversify the applicant pool, then you can make friction a more visible, more real phenomena. Highlighting the sources of friction can also provide direction in removing them.

Once you get everyone to see the problem, there are other sources of friction to manage. It is incredibly challenging to get people to go beyond initial implementation to long-term execution. A new diversity and inclusion initiative can be launched with enthusiasm and good intent, but once it is out of the spotlight, it can fade away.

So, how do we resolve friction points so that we can create a system that is optimized for success? A critical starting point for identifying and eliminating friction is to look within ourselves as a potential source of friction.

INTROSPECTION

You are reading this book, so we believe that diversity and inclusion is important to you, and you are interested in making a difference in your organization. You want information and we're glad you are here to receive it. We believe that to find solutions to pressing problems, those problems—in full—must be revealed.

Questions we need to ask to create opportunities for equality in our workplace environment include:

- Why do diversity and inclusion initiatives fall short of their intended outcome so frequently?

- How is it that efforts to reduce tension and create equality often have an opposite effect, effectively creating more tension?

- What are the ways we can prevent "diversity fatigue" when those who support diversity and inclusion reach their burnout points?

- What can we do when the problem seems too hard to solve?

Maria Morukian states in an article published by *Forbes*, "Part of the struggle to embrace inclusion is that we human beings are not hardwired for it. We instinctively seek safety, stability, and similarity. We protect ourselves from anything we perceive as a threat—to our beliefs, way of life, or sense of self." (Morukian, 2020). This means we need to address what is happening inward to be effective in outward initiatives. So championing diversity and inclusion requires honest introspection. That is a pretty scary thought for folks who have an inkling of their own biases. Yet moving forward without acknowledging and managing one's own biases can reduce the integrity of your position. Here, I will borrow Landmark Education's definition of integrity. Their definition of integrity is not as firmly tied to moral uprightness or doing the "right" thing. For them, and for me, it has more to do with authenticity—being true to ourselves—and it is the foundation for power and effectiveness. It is a home, an anchor, a continuing commitment—a way of being and acting that shapes who we are. When we operate from this type of integrity, it hits differently. It is not a preachy, holier-than-thou positioning. It is being true to yourself, acknowledging your flaws, and allowing others to engage from wherever they are.

This is necessary because no one person or team can make inclusion mainstream. Let's say that again: *No one person or team can make inclusion mainstream.* Owning your flaws makes it easier for others to engage with you as you do inclusion work. It takes the collective to bring the work to its fullest potential.

THE OPPORTUNITY

You have now taken a dive into some of the most important topics related to the setbacks of diversity and inclusion in the business environment. This means you have more in-depth knowledge of:

- Bias: What terms and assumptions do you use that create a wedge between you and others, particularly in terms of race and gender equality?

- A Contract with Humanity: How is human decency perceived differently by different races? It is easy to note the imbalance of just outcomes between people of color and Caucasians.

- White Fragility: People are not often able to point out their own biases on their own. It requires us to engage in thinking and reflection that goes beyond what we currently do to see the inequalities that exist due to a lack of comfort and fear of shaking up a system that works for some but not for all.

- Hidden Friction in Organizations: It does not matter how much you support diversity and inclusion or even if you tried it in your organization; it's going against the friction and keeping on moving forward to completion that makes the difference people are seeking.

- Introspection: In a world where good intentions often burn out after people lose their energy and drive to put up the good fight, we need to ensure that we look inward to have a solid foundation. Without integrity, we will not have the stamina required for the long fight ahead.

Once you know something needs to change, what do you do? We love poet Dr. Maya Angelou's view on this question and believe it ought to have a higher place in the minds of business leaders. "When you know better, do better."

We know enough now to do as Maya instrusted; so much better. In the next chapter, we cover the roles that data transparency, reputation management, and the free flow of information play in this pursuit.

CHAPTER THREE

ON DATA-DRIVEN DIVERSITY AND INCLUSION

D ata tells a story that every business needs to listen to. It is a trigger to learning more. We have both had a lot of experience working with small businesses in our work with entrepreneurial service organizations, those (usually nonprofit or governmental) organizations set up to help emerging business owners. While working with one such organization, we got to work with lots of folks who are passionate about helping entrepreneurs. One of our team members was a helpful front desk worker whose primary role was to greet visitors, conduct tours, and make sure that the immediate needs of the founders who worked in the space were handled. This woman was masterful at her role at the front desk, which included a hospitality element. After taking time to learn more about her, we realized that she was a veteran business owner. This meant she had a wealth of experiences and situations she'd handled in order to keep her business afloat. When we learned more about her, she was encouraged to apply to become a business advisor. She thrived in the role and brought a great deal more value to the organization as a result.

The important part of this story is that we shifted our perception of this woman who had entered the organization as a frontline worker. By engaging in a conversation, we found out that she had a wealth of knowledge that could help to elevate the clients that the organization serves. The lesson we learned that informed our data-driven approach to inclusion is that we could have uncovered her potential even sooner if we'd collected data about everyone who applies and enters the organization. Had we set up our systems to look for experience and expertise with everyone, not just those entering our organization through specialized pathways, we could have optimized the potential of our talent pool.

Did you know that one of Frito-Lay's most successful product launches came from an unexpected source of talent within their organization? Richard Montañez rose from a janitor making $4 an hour plus benefits to PepsiCo executive after inventing Flamin' Hot Cheetos. Montañez dropped out of school in the fourth grade, worked as a migrant farmer, and had enough of a struggle with literacy that his wife helped him to fill out his application to work as a janitor with Frito-Lay. He created the Flamin' Hot Cheeto after a broken machine on the Cheetos assembly line spit out a batch of plain Cheetos, without the cheese powder dust. Montañez took the Cheetos home and dusted them with chili powder. Montañez was inspired by *elotes*, a popular spicy Mexican grilled corn sold by street vendors. He first pitched the idea to former PepsiCo CEO Roger Enrico over the phone and was given two weeks to prepare a presentation to the executive suite. It was tested in Los Angeles six months later and rolled out nationally in 1992. Flamin' Hot Cheetos has generated billions in revenue since launch. Montañez was named vice president of multicultural sales and community promotions for PepsiCo (the parent company of Frito-Lay). His story has been the subject of two books, and a movie to be directed by Eva Longoria and produced by DeVon Franklin is in the works (Whalen, 2019).

Richard Montañez's extraordinary story teaches us about how organizations can reap the rewards of allowing everyone to be heard. Frito-Lay and PepsiCo have a culture that provides a competitive advantage.

Later, we will explore how data can be used to uncover areas of inequity in an organization, but we wanted to start by highlighting upside opportunities. Diversity and inclusion data can be a great tool to illuminate potential; it's not just for indicating where an organization is weak. We will discuss how to use data for opportunity in later chapters.

The need for data has increased greatly over the years, and across all industries and sectors, including government policy making.

At the outset of the pandemic, city leaders in Chicago used data to discover an ugly fact: among those for whom race-ethnicity is known, 72% of the city's deaths have been among black Chicagoans, though black Chicagoans make up just 30% of the city's population. Data also showed a frightening and disproportionate increase in cases among Latinx residents. Looking at undeniable data helped Chicago Mayor Lori Lightfoot take serious and decisive action quickly.

She created the Chicago Racial Equity Rapid Response Team, and named the city's first chief equity officer as a point person in charge. The main purpose of the initiative is to develop hyperlocal, data-informed strategies to combat the spread of COVID-19 and improve health outcomes among Black and Brown communities, Chicago's most heavily impacted (Whalen, 2019).

In the business world, the need and the demand for data to tell us a revealing picture about diversity and inclusion is just as urgent. This is what data can tell us:

- How cultural shifts impact diversity and inclusion

- How and in what way inclusion can influence productivity

- What are the areas of opportunity to increase innovation through inclusion

Overall, society has more ease and comfort with documentation than any previous time. Platforms like social media enable viral content to surface that changes lives and how businesses must operate. There is generally a low tolerance for the poor treatment of employees or trying to sweep diversity and inclusion issues under the rug.

We are also part of a society where employees have shorter stays at their jobs. The result is less loyalty to a specific employer and more loyalty to personal growth and opportunities. How employers responded to COVID-19 with their frontline workers is a prime example of this. Those organizations that did not treat these workers well will find a harsher reality on the other side of the pandemic, measured by a decrease in employee retention and productivity. If they want to maintain their talent and optimize their results, they will be required to change.

DATA AND THE FREE FLOW OF INFORMATION

Data is key to all change. When it is evaluated as it is, data is void of emotion. It provides information to create a story. Storytelling is where perception and emotion come in.

A profound example of the power of data transparency took place on March 3, 1991, when a Black motorist named Rodney King was pulled over by police and brutally beaten. To anyone who recalls this, they are aware of what a disturbing situation it was.

When it comes to data and the free flow of information, this incident has further impact. It was the first time that a police beating of an unarmed Black person was caught on camera and widely distributed. It set a public precedent for acts that took place against African Americans by police officers and shifted the narrative around police in a profound way.

Today, many of our public activities and even some of our private deeds can be caught on camera, which has implications for our personal reputations and for the organizations and people with whom we are affiliated. Because people produce content all the time, there is an endless flow of information and an expectation that the information is available for easy perusal for anyone with basic Google search skills. That data can be posted to social media accounts where it can be scrutinized and judged. There is no more doing something and then it slowly fades away as the memory fades. This content remains active for people to analyze and even distort to support their position.

This dynamic has implications for how data is used and presented. Recognize that there are multiple and sometimes conflicting perspectives. People will interpret data in a variety of ways to meet their needs, based on their biases. And there is also an expectation that data is present, accessible, and available. This is driven by the rise of the quantified self. The quantified self refers both to the cultural phenomenon of self-tracking with technology and to a community of users and makers of self-tracking tools who share an interest in self-knowledge through numbers and data combined with some measure of performative activity and documentation. From Fitbit step trackers to Instagram posts, we generate an endless flow of information for consumption by an audience that is both real and imagined.

It is totally reasonable today to know how many steps you walked each day, how many calories you burned each month, how many cities you visited each year, and how many people liked your photos. For many people, peeling back the layers on themselves and their environments has created an expectation of transparency of other things that were previously unknown. People want to know where their food is coming from, the political leanings of the owners of the businesses they frequent, and the diversity and inclusion of the companies they support. How we manage this demand has the potential to create a significant positive or negative impact on an organization's reputation.

DATA-DRIVEN DIVERSITY AND INCLUSION ENGAGEMENT

Being data-driven in your engagement with other organizations can provide needed clarity on the alignment between stated values, practiced behavior, and realized outcomes. Weremember working with a nonprofit organization that was seeking funding from the Kapor Center. Founded by Mitch Kapor, the creator of Lotus 123 (predecessor to Microsoft Excel) and his wife Dr. Freada Kapor Klein, the Kapor Center's mission is to level the playing field in technology. The organization that we worked for was interested in getting support from the Kapor Center for its diversity- and inclusion-focused programming that helps underrepresented tech founders. In previous applications, our organization had successfully positioned itself as a champion of inclusion. This was because those applications did not have any clear parameters to qualify an organization as inclusive. The Kapor Center included the following item in their application.

Please indicate if your organization fits any of the following categories (Check all that apply).

☐ At least 50 percent of the board is comprised of people of color

☐ At least 50 percent of staff is comprised of people of color

☐ Executive Director or CEO is a person of color

☐ This grant request focuses on communities of color

☐ None of the above

The data did not lie. We were working for an organization that had a strong will to be seen as inclusive. They felt they were doing the right things. Yet despite the fact that they were in a community that was over 80 percent Black, 75 percent of their senior leadership team was White. Their majority-White staff didn't at all reflect the community they served. The grant request did focus on communities of color. While the organization talked the talk about a commitment to inclusion, it clearly did not walk the walk. This was a very illuminating moment for the staff because it was a point in which the data exposed the truth about who we actually were, not who we said we were.

Organizations that operate in integrity align what they say with what they do.

This incident started a conversation at our organization that started to lead to real change. Change was not a matter of firing all the White people and replacing them with Black people. The process of change took time to develop. A key component was intentional succession. Most of our fellow team members do not intend to stay at the organization for more than a few years, so it gave leadership the opportunity to talk about change through attrition. The radical idea of employees discussing their internal timetables for leaving with their bosses was a part of the planning process.

Intentional succession aids recruitment of a diverse team. If it is clear that management is intentionally making room at the leadership table for people of color, it attracts high-potential people seeking opportunity. This methodology offers long-term value. You will not be able to keep everyone you want on your team forever, but you can retain people for a longer time because more people are attracted to your organization. You can also expect that those people are more likely to offer their best work because they feel valued and accepted.

EMPLOYEE LOYALTY IN THE AGE OF THE FREE AGENT

We are living in a world where people are less likely to be loyal to an employer for the long term. Workers change jobs on average every 4.2 years, according to the Bureau of Labor Statistics. There is a stark generational difference. The median tenure of workers ages twenty-five to thirty-four is 2.8 years, compared with 10.1 years for workers ages fifty-five to sixty-four.

Marlor's first job after earning my undergraduate degree was as a salesperson with Kellogg. She started just in time to attend the company-wide sales meeting in Orlando, Florida. She remembers seeing the retirement ceremonies for a number of people in the organization. One man was given a gold watch for fifty years of service. Upon receiving it, he tearfully exclaimed that he wished he had fifty more years to give to the company. She turned to the other new hires and recalls everyone looking at each other with a "shoot me if I ever say anything that crazy" look.

As Generation Xers, we were the first generation to be a part of the workplace shift from lifetime employment to free agency. Millennials and Gen Z professionals have the dynamic of personal branding and social media influence that has added more of a power dynamic for visible high earners in key positions-or even for those interested in raising their profile. On any given day, LinkedIn posts with professionals making career announcements is common-place. Those with more storied careers change careers with all of the drama of an NBA trade. Reputation management now means that your company can now appear as a hero or villain in any of these stories.

Consider the story of Bozoma "Badass Boz" Saint John, marketing wunderkind and cultural tastemaker. Born in Connecticut to Ghanaian parents, she went from pre-med undergrad to model to land her first marketing job with Spike Lee's advertising firm, Spike DDB. She was a music promoter in college, bringing a young Jay-Z to her alma mater, Wesleyan. She taught a class on Tupac Shakur as well. She worked on five projects with Beyoncé during her decade-long tenure as the head of music and entertainment marketing at Pepsi. Ultimately, she parlayed her deep pop culture roots and marketing expertise to be the head of global consumer marketing for iTunes and Apple Music. She was chief brand officer at Uber and became chief marketing officer at Netflix in 2020 (Whalen, 2019).

Bozoma's career trajectory, particularly her transition from her role at Uber only one year into her tenure, is an example of how high-profile hires and exits can impact an organization's reputation. She created and maintained a personal brand that was not tied to any specific job; one that influences–even in a small way–her former corporation upon her exit. As more individuals gain fluency on how to create influence via social media, they can and will start wielding their power to shape the story of their work experience from their perspective. Organizations who don't know how to make these individuals feel included will lose the competition for great talent. Companies that are actively discriminatory will risk much more significant losses.

When Nike took its controversial stand to support and elevate former NFL quarterback and social justice icon Colin Kaepernick, it isolated some customers and gained loyalty from its base. Kaepernick was the lead endorser for the 30th anniversary of Nike's "Just Do It" brand motto, which generated global headlines and inspired a Harvard Business School case study. Taking that stand was a risk, but one that affirmed the values of Nike's most loyal customers–customers whose values are rarely acknowledged by corporations, much less uplifted.

As Marlin says, "People feel supported by the values reflected in an organization." They meet these needs based on perception, knowing they will move on when they feel their needs can be met elsewhere better. And when someone else is perceived as "better," you become perceived as "worse," and word gets out.

You want people to be an ambassador for you, first and foremost. If they are sharing on their Facebook page or Instagram, you want them to share authentically good stuff. Because they will write what they feel.

INDICATORS FOR INCLUSION

When she was the head of diversity and inclusion at Blend, Ciara Gonzalez-Trinidad understood how data can help to build accountability and guide key results. When she worked for Lever as the head of diversity and inclusion, she was able to achieve impressive results. The start-up's team of 125 people was 59 percent women, 39 percent men, and 2 percent gender nonconforming. Even the sales team was a 50/50-split.

How did it happen? As Gonzalez-Trinidad noted, "It was a combination of project-management chops and a passion for doing the work." Have this and you have an opportunity.

Having the data gives you the details to create the narrative that will move your organization forward in a manner that aligns with diversity and inclusion. This is scary, isn't it? How can you be sure your data reveals the best story? What steps can you take to have a favorable outcome?

Using metrics and performance indicators gives you the insights to make the best decisions based on where your business currently is and where you know your business needs to go.

Let's explore how metrics and performance indicators can push you through the challenges and on to better organizational structure and results.

Everybody discusses the importance of data but it is rendered useless if you do not know how to interpret it and use it to build true diversity and inclusion—and stop just saying it matters.

Gonzalez-Trinidad said this about data: "I rely really heavily on data. Diversity professionals might read that and roll their eyes, because we've *all* been working on data. But it's more than just using the data behind the scenes. It's about presenting the data to every party that has a stake in the game." (First Round Review, n.d.).

Steps to evaluate data clearly and precisely include:

- Create a dashboard to consolidate data in a clear and digestible way

- Present information to stakeholders so they understand it

These metrics are then used to fix the problem at hand. Your first thought may be, "Well, we'll just tell the recruiters to adjust this for hiring." This is not the approach that will work. Instead, you need to engage them in the conversation, combining their area of expertise with the data's story. This is how you build a narrative of what your numbers represent and where they could be.

From there, you need to look at each department, analyzing the numbers and the context over time, then build your story in a way that acknowledges each department as a group and acknowledges how they fit into the larger organization.

This is done through the diversity dashboard. Why do it? Because it shows people managers what is actually going on and allows them to start asking specific questions that lead to problems being solved.

Discussions are what give the muscle to the data you are evaluating. The conversation is where the real change begins.

THE DETAILS ARE ON THE DASHBOARD

The best way to view your diversity dashboard is as a product. This means it is important to view it like a product manager. Ask what the problem is you want the tool to solve? Then, find a concrete story to explain why. This is what will support all the trends and data you find through using the dashboard.

After this, you will educate yourself on where your organization's data is stored. Mostly you can find this with Human Resources, likely in the information system. You may also have this information laid out in a spreadsheet if you don't have an information system. Evaluate the data asking these questions:

- Is this all the data?

- Does it live in my applicant tracking system?

- How much qualitative data sits in the software I use for performance reviews?

These are steps that often require partnering with a specialist in data interpretation to complete. You need to not only view the data but understand it too.

The dashboard samples that we highlight below are good benchmarks. It is important to note that we did not assist in their creation.

Below is an example of Intuit's diversity and inclusion dashboard.

The dashboard is here: *https://www.ceoaction.com/ media/2521/intuit-di-dashboard.jpg.*

The pay equity and pulse results charts tell a particularly compelling story of the results of the company's efforts to engage women team members.

Next, you will determine which data points are relevant to the questions you're investigating. Don't overwhelm and inundate yourself with too much data. Use only that which applies. For example:

- Gender

- Birth date

- Parental status

- Race

Fig 1. Intuit diversity and inclusion dashboard

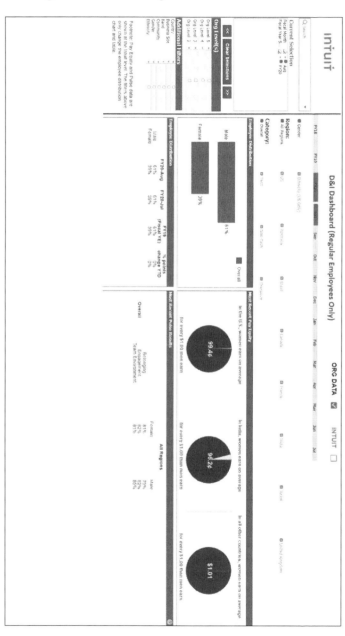

- Veteran status

- Differently abled

- Tenure

- Department

These eight metrics are highly relevant and can help you find a meaningful narrative within your dashboard. NOTE: never add names to the field of metrics because you don't want names associated with the data.

With all the data in tow, it's time to organize it into a story. You may need to play around with various queries to discover which are most revealing. Here are three that are revealing in what they relay:

- **Hires by month by team:** This shows how recruiters fare against diversity and inclusion strategies, as well as the way their recruiting environment works.

- **Hires by month by race:** This data is likely to surface your organization's internal biases but also their interplay with the industry's hiring. If the ratio of hiring is skewed, we need to know why. It isn't always bad, but what are the reasons that it is the way it is.

- **Hires by tenure:** Start dates and end dates can yield a wealth of information, too. Often, those numbers contain valuable feedback regarding missed opportunities. You can also look at gender, race, and parental status to determine reasons these people may be leaving the organization.

The city of Cambridge, Massachusetts, has a robust dashboard for tracking its employee trends. It is designed to provide a great deal of information quickly, through effective visual design.

The dashboard is here: *https://www.cambridgema.gov/ departments/equityandinclusion/interactiveequityand-inclusiondashboard.*

Using these tools to make data more easily searchable allows you to look at numbers in a more revealing way. You can narrow them down to departments more easily, for example. In either case, the data helps you determine your next steps.

CREATING YOUR DASHBOARD STORY

A leader in diversity and inclusion isn't meant to interpret data on their own. This is because while your dashboard is crucial, reviewing it with relevant stakeholders is what makes it invaluable.

The best idea to help the narrative, conversation, and change move forward is to hold a regular meeting with hiring managers and their recruiters. This is how you learn what's happening on the front line and can share your

Fig 2. Cambridge employee demographics dashboard

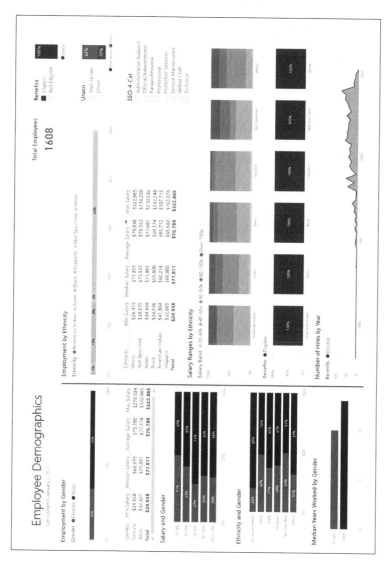

data with them. Everyone feels like they are a part of the conversation because they are. We're all in this together.

During these meetings the most common two questions asked are:

- Where is the data from?

- How am I impacting the results?

Answering where it is from will depend on your reporting sources. Make sure that your data sources are ones that the leaders you engage believe are accurate. If the leaders you engage with at your company don't believe your data is accurate, it will be a major source of contention. What people really want to know is how they impact these results and what the results mean to them, or even about them.

For example, if you are a hiring manager or the deciding factor in a hiring choice, you need to be sure that your reasonings for your decisions are not rooted in bias. And if they are, this is not something to take personally. It is often due to being unaware of it or following the flow of a larger, company or industry wide culture. Without sharing the data, these people do not realize change is needed. This is why the data is so important.

After these meetings, the team should have a way to review and return to the information presented. It's up to you, the one delivering the data, to provide them with something, whether it's a bullet point list of talking points or ongoing access to the dashboard.

Foster a culture of data mindfulness and the data will work better for you.

OPEN FOR CONVERSATION

To start the conversation on diversity and inclusion, you have to first tackle one big challenge: getting management to admit this is new and unfamiliar. This can be hard to admit. Yet, it is an important step to take. Then education and action can begin.

Candor, combined with education, is a powerful way to grow a team that values diversity and inclusion. Let's not forget the cultural shift, either, because when this is in place, the culture is bound to change. Instead of whispering we have a 4 percent Black hire rate, it can be said out loud because it's not an end goal, it's a factual number that you are working with. Admitting where you are and where you wish to go out loud takes away the stigma and builds traction to what you want to achieve. Diversity and inclusion isn't a private conversation, it is an initiative with shared responsibility across a corporation. People need to speak freely to assess progress and determine next steps.

Leadership being on board with diversity and inclusion initiatives and having their doors open to be available to make a difference is key. The best way to accomplish this is to have a chief diversity and inclusion officer reporting to the CEO. That person needs to be able to engage in authentic and powerful conversations in which people feel safe (though not always comfortable) and heard.

Be prepared to answer and guide people with questions that matter. Expect to hear:

- Why is it so important?

- Who do I think this is going to help?

- How do I bring people along with me?

- How do I make sure that everybody understands this is what we're doing, and why?

When you share your next steps, you will want to tell everyone what it means and how it will impact the business. When you talk through how an inclusive culture is a good business move, you usually find people want to participate and be more accepting. They just need to understand why.

As you lay out these initiatives just start wherever you can. Every business has a different starting point but starting is what matters most. It's the baseline for gauging improvement. It also gives you an opportunity to lay out what success will look like when it's achieved.

Undertaking this entire process is a daunting task for someone without experience as a diversity and inclusion professional, which means bringing in the experts will matter. They can train current staff and help put together policies that will carry your business into the future.

DIVERSITY AND INCLUSION MANAGEMENT IS A SKILL

All this change needs to be made and wants to be made. Who takes the lead? This is best done by tapping an expert, whether he or she is internal or external to the company. That person should engage with people across the organization. It is important to recognize that diversity and inclusion work requires specific skill. It is not something you are qualified to do simply because you want to see it done. You wouldn't expect someone to become a chief financial officer without financial training. There is no shortage of diversity and inclusion training opportunities and certifications available.

No matter what level of expertise is brought to bear, nothing substantive can be done without company-wide commitment and resources. There should be broad buy-in, including people from recruiting, engineering, sales, and marketing—these people can lay the groundwork for success.

Go in with clear expectations and realize you won't get everything done right away. Mistakes will happen. This is why you need the support of your team. If you all are joined in on a great end goal, the process will be less chaotic when mistakes are made and you will be better able to appreciate what goes right along the way. And remember, it is okay to screw up if you are also willing to resolve what went wrong.

Another "must do" step is to offer some type of financial compensation and appropriate increase in authority to those who are undergoing these important, corporate and culture changing initiatives. Especially if you are not hiring diversity and inclusion as a full-time job. People's work needs to be valued or they will become a part of your problems, not your solutions. It will destroy your culture if your employees feel like your diversity and inclusion initiatives have been built on their backs.

Also, never have the head of human resources be your diversity lead. Ciara Gonzalez-Trinidad put it this way: "If you conflate human resources and diversity and inclusion, you immediately set up a conflict of interest."

Marlin believes this from years of experience and says it often. "Diversity and inclusion should not be relegated to human resources (HR). Diversity and inclusion is a whole business strategy, not a human resources program." She believes that it's HR's job to protect the company. It's diversity and inclusion's job to protect the people. That's not to say that they'll always be at odds. HR and diversity and inclusion will often need to collaborate. But their respective responsibilities are too incompatible to be combined. HR may be focused on areas such as compensation, benefits and recruiting. Diversity and inclusion is thinking about the things you're bringing into the organization from home, the cultural appropriation you've had to deal with, the fact that you're a single mother.

This is also one of the reasons that some organizations hire from the outside. They can come in with a fresh perspective on diversity and inclusion, evaluate data, and progress from there.

THE OPPORTUNITY

We know the power of data to inform and expose us. It can highlight injustice, hypocrisy, and bias. It can illuminate opportunity and focus effort. It creates an opportunity for a powerful story to be revealed, and for that story to make an impact.

Reputation management has become more crucial for business than ever before. Data is the raw material that, when shaped through skillful storytelling and guided by authenticity and integrity, helps to forge a reputation that is an asset rather than a liability.

Much of what you can do to start implementing diversity and inclusion initiatives begins with the data you have and one of two choices:

1. Use data to change perceptions about diversity and inclusion

2. Use data to support perceptions about diversity and inclusion

An organization usually contains people from both perspectives. From this point you can begin to explore strategy.

- Find relevant metrics to use in order to gauge where your organization currently stands regarding diversity and inclusion in your culture.

- You need to accumulate a group of individuals who are willing to help you brainstorm possible solutions, as well as bring together viewpoints from their specific roles within the organization.

- Determine if you need to hire an outside consulting firm for this initiative or if you have enough employees where it can be an internal position. Remember the "big rule"-- the head of human resources is not the person that should be in charge of a diversity and inclusion program. They deal with separate issues.

- Get the opinions of a broad range of people. Having others vested in the diversity and inclusion directive will give the effort support and increase its chances of success.

But what happens when the data shows an ongoing and persistent problem at your organization. And what happens when you investigate that problem and can only conclude that the organization is fundamentally unable to support inclusion. Before we address that issue, we need to explore the origins and purpose of diversity and inclusion work in corporations.

CHAPTER FOUR

ON THE INCLUSION IMPERATIVE

One of the most common misunderstandings about diversity is that it is synonymous with affirmative action. Affirmative action is rooted in an effort at the federal level to combat discriminatory practices. Diversity and inclusion initiatives were designed as voluntary programs to strive toward fixing racial and gender imbalances in the workplace. Diversity today also takes a broader and more inclusive view, welcoming sexual orientation, cultural and ethnic heritage, and ability difference. Diversity and inclusion professionals recognize that there are direct business benefits to inclusive practices and work to maximize them.

AFFIRMATIVE ACTION AND DIVERSITY: HISTORY AND KEY DISTINCTIONS

Knowing the history and distinctions between affirmative action and diversity, at least in part, is crucial to ensuring effective policy is created. Below is a timeline of historic milestones related to affirmative action (CNN Editorial Research, 2020).

- **1954 –** The US Supreme Court, in *Brown v. Board of Education*, rules that the "separate but equal" doctrine violates the Constitution.

- **1961 –** President Kennedy creates the Council on Equal Opportunity in an executive order. This ensures that federal contractors hire people regardless of race, creed, color or national origin.

- **1964 –** The Civil Rights Act renders discrimination illegal in the workplace.

- **1978 –** In *Regents of the University of California v. Bakke*, a notable reverse discrimination case, the Supreme Court rules that colleges cannot use racial quotas because it violates the Equal Protection Clause. As one factor for admission, however, race can be used.

- **1995 –** The University of Michigan rejects the college application of Jennifer Gratz, a top high school student in suburban Detroit who is white.

October 14, 1997 – *Gratz v. Bollinger, et al.*, is filed in federal court in the Eastern District of Michigan. The University of Michigan is sued by white students, including Gratz and Patrick Hamacher, who claim the undergraduate and law school affirmative action policies using race and/or gender as a factor in admissions is a violation of the Equal Protection Clause of the Fourteenth Amendment or Title VI of the Civil Rights Act of 1964.

December 3, 1997 – A similar case, *Grutter v. Bollinger*, is filed in federal court in the Eastern District of Michigan. Barbara Grutter, denied admission to the University of Michigan Law School, claims that other applicants, with lower test scores and grades, were given an unfair advantage due to race.

December 2000 – The judge in the *Gratz v. Bollinger* case rules that the University of Michigan's undergraduate admissions policy does not violate the standards set by the Supreme Court.

March 2001 – The judge in the *Grutter v. Bollinger* case rules the University of Michigan Law School's admissions policy is unconstitutional.

December 2001 – The Sixth Circuit Court of Appeals hears appeals in both University of Michigan cases.

May 14, 2002 - The Sixth Circuit Court of Appeals reverses the district court's decision in *Grutter v. Bollinger*.

January 17, 2003 - The administration of President George W. Bush files a friend-of-the-court brief with the Supreme Court, opposing the University of Michigan's affirmative action program.

April 1, 2003 - The US Supreme Court hears oral arguments on the two cases. US Solicitor General Theodore Olson offers arguments in support of the plaintiffs.

June 23, 2003 - The Supreme Court rules on *Grutter v. Bollinger* that the University of Michigan Law School may give preferential treatment to minorities during the admissions process. The Court upholds the law school policy by a vote of five to four.

June 23, 2003 - In *Gratz v. Bollinger*, the undergraduate policy in which a point system gave specific "weight" to minority applicants is overturned six to three.

December 22, 2003 - The Supreme Court rules that race can be a factor in universities' admission programs but it cannot be an overriding factor. This decision affects the Grutter and Gratz cases.

November 7, 2006 - The Michigan electorate strikes down affirmative action by approving a proposition barring affirmative action in public education, employment, or contracting.

January 31, 2007 - After the Supreme Court sends the case back to district court; the case is dismissed. Gratz and Hamacher settle for $10,000 in administrative costs, but do not receive damages.

2008 - Abigail Noel Fisher, a white woman, sues the University of Texas. She argues that the university should not use race as a factor in admission policies that favor African-American and Hispanic applicants over whites and Asian Americans.

July 1, 2011 - An appeals court overturns Michigan's 2006 ban on the use of race and/or gender as a factor in admissions or hiring practices.

November 15, 2012 - The US Sixth Circuit Court of Appeals throws out Michigan's 2006 ban on affirmative action in college admissions and public hiring, declaring it unconstitutional.

June 24, 2013 - The Supreme Court sends the University of Texas case back to the lower court for further review without ruling.

October 15, 2013 - The US Supreme Court hears oral arguments in a case concerning Michigan's 2006 law on affirmative action.

- **April 22, 2014 -** In a six to two ruling, the Supreme Court upholds Michigan's ban on using racial criteria in college admissions.

- **July 15, 2014 -** The US Court of Appeals for the Fifth Circuit upholds the use of race by the University of Texas as a factor in undergraduate admissions to promote diversity on campus. The vote is two to one.

- **November 17, 2014 -** Students for Fair Admissions sues Harvard University, alleging Harvard intentionally discriminates against Asian Americans. Students for Fair Admissions is run by Edward Blum, a conservative advocate, who sought Asian Americans rejected by Harvard.

- **December 9, 2015 -** The US Supreme Court hears oral arguments in the University of Texas case regarding race as a factor in admissions policies.

- **June 23, 2016 -** The US Supreme Court upholds the Affirmative Action program by a vote of four to three with Justice Elena Kagan taking no part in the consideration. The ruling allows the limited use of affirmative action policies by schools.

- **October 15, 2018 -** The lawsuit against Harvard filed in 2014 by Students for Fair Admissions goes to trial.

February 2019 – Texas Tech University enters an agreement with the Department of Education to stop considering race and/or national origin as a factor in its admissions process, concluding a 14-year-long investigation into the school's use of affirmative action.

October 1, 2019 – US District Court Judge Allison Burroughs upholds Harvard's admissions process in the Students for Fair Admissions case, ruling that while Harvard's admissions process is "not perfect," she would not "dismantle a very fine admissions program that passes constitutional muster, solely because it could do better."

November 12, 2020 – A Boston-based US appeals court rejects an appeal brought by the Students for Fair Admissions group.

Diversity and inclusion initiatives in the workplace got their start in 1948 when President Truman signed Executive Order 9981, desegregating the military. The Civil Rights Act of 1964 made it illegal for any business, private or public, to practice discriminatory hiring.

In 1987, US Secretary of Labor William Brock commissioned a study of economic and demographic trends. The findings became Workforce 2000–Work and Workers for the Twenty-first Century. This book was a benchmark that informed and guided corporate diversity policy since its publishing. Workforce 2000 highlighted five demographic factors that would impact the US labor market (Johnston & Packer, 1987).

1. The population and the workforce will grow more slowly than at any time since the 1930s.

2. The average age of the population and the workforce will rise, and the pool of young workers entering the labor market will shrink.

3. More women will enter the workforce.

4. Minorities will be a larger share of the new entrants into the labor force.

5. Legal and illegal immigrants will represent the largest share of the increase in the population and the workforce since World War I.

Some companies recognized the business opportunity represented by these trends. In order to attract workers and remain competitive, companies started to invest in diversity initiatives. Companies sought to measure diversity in terms of turnover, retention, productivity, succession planning, public image, revenue/market share and stock value. Diversity initiatives were broadened dramatically to include flexible schedules, emergency daycare, flexibility in dress requirements, nonstandard career paths, phased retirement and domestic partner benefits. Diversity has evolved since that time to focus on inclusion, belonging, and equity, rather than diversity, as markers for success.

Today, diversity policies can be unevenly implemented and widely maligned. From our standpoint, if diversity and inclusion initiatives are performative efforts to dodge accountability and create real change, then they are at best useless and more likely fraudulent. Companies with persistent patterns of discriminatory behavior sometimes hire a diversity and inclusion figurehead after their practices have been exposed. The person who takes on that role becomes little more than a more sympathetic apologist than the company leaders.

Ultimately, a sincere focus on inclusion requires implementation of initiatives as an integral component of a company's strategic practice. Understanding diversity and inclusion as a means for accomplishing your objectives and key results helps to drive implementation. Investment in the diversity and inclusion function and a direct connection to the CEO are hallmarks of authentic, meaningful execution.

THE POST-PANDEMIC EMERGENCE OF INCLUSION INITIATIVES

The COVID-19 pandemic and racial reckoning of 2020 brought with them a wave of inclusion initiatives at several well-known corporations. Companies made significant public investments and hires in response to an increased awareness of inequity and more pressure to make real change, with mixed results.

Google CEO Sundar Pichai announced a $310-million commitment to fund a council to oversee diversity and equality issues as part of a shareholder lawsuit settlement over mishandling of sexual misconduct by company executives. "I hope these commitments will serve as a strong signal to all of you that we are not going back in time," Pichai wrote to employees and shareholders troubled by the company's policies on treatment of allegations of misconduct and harassment (Johnston & Packer, 1987). Later, Google's high-profile employee separations with Black computer scientist Dr. Timnit Gebru and Black diversity recruiter April Christina Curley were dramatic and problematic departures played out in the media and on social media (Glaser, 2020).

The publishing giant Condé Nast named its first global chief diversity and inclusion officer in 2020. Starbucks decided to tie all executive pay to a demonstrable effort to achieve a new diversity target of 30 percent Black, indigneous and people of color employees at its corporate level by 2025. At the retail level, Starbucks set a diversity goal of 40 percent.

The new initiative will be tied to pay starting with the 2021 fiscal year. Along with linking executive pay to diversity, Starbucks pledged to embed anti-bias content into all of its hiring, development and performance processes.

Leaders at the vice president level will be required to complete anti-bias and anti-racist courses. In early 2020, Goldman Sachs pledged to require at least one non-White male board member on any client company that it takes public.

These investments in inclusion are driven by the imperative to maximize shareholder value. There are real, potentially long-term consequences to having a company culture that is not inclusive.

One example of the impact of a negative culture can be found by observing Uber. Uber's rapid and tumultuous growth over the ten years between its founding and IPO is tied to the dynamics of its culture. Uber has grown to be one of the most valuable companies in the world, but it has also fired over twenty employees over sexual harassment allegations. It has paid out millions in discrimination settlements. Its cofounder Travis Kalanick resigned as CEO under mounting public pressure, and it lost hundreds of millions in market capitalization as a result.

Another company on our radar for diversity and inclusion lapses is Pepsi. In 2017, they produced a commercial that featured Kendall Jenner. It showed Ms. Jenner taking a break from a photo shoot and jumping into a protest against police. The conflict was ultimately resolved when Ms. Jenner shared a Pepsi with one of the officers. The ad, produced by Pepsi's in-house content creation arm, was widely seen to have appropriated the Black Lives Matter movement. The backlash played out on traditional and social media. Pepsi deleted the content and apologized to everyone involved. We can't help but to believe that a more inclusive team may have had members on it with an understanding of the issues involved in the commercial content and the agency to make their perspectives known.

THE FIVE BUSINESS NEEDS

Diversity and inclusion are basic building blocks for the effective management of organizations. People from a wide range of backgrounds make better and more productive teams, particularly if those teams are addressing problems or opportunities on a global scale or with some deep level of complexity. Inclusion is an imperative because it can be leveraged to help organizations meet five fundamental needs that are critical components for ongoing success.

The five business needs are listed below.

1. **The need for great talent.** When organizations move beyond diversity to inclusion, they can access deep pools of talent that can bring fresh ideas and innovation.

2. **The need for innovative product/service development.** The range of viewpoints and experiences of people from different backgrounds and perspectives can help create some of the most forward moving and innovative products and services.

3. **The need to understand an increasingly diverse set of customers.** High growth, scalable businesses by definition have a large customer base. An inclusive organization is better positioned to understand the multiple cultures and subcultures within that base.

4. **The need for flexible, cost-conscious supply chain management.** A diverse supplier base enables greater flexibility, spreads and mitigates risk, provides cost-saving alternatives, and promotes innovation.

5. **The need for solid operations practices.** Creating teams with cohesiveness of practices and expectations allows for people to work in a customer's best interests, as well as make sure that they are not being taken advantage of in some manner.

Inclusion can help managers run their businesses better in all of these areas under normal business conditions

TIMES OF CRISIS

A time of crisis is a time of need, a situation that changes life forevermore. COVID-19 proved itself to be such a crisis. Even now.

People will remember how they were treated by you during this time. Those on the front lines will recall exactly what it felt like working for a company during such a challenging time. It wasn't only difficult on many businesses; it was also difficult on people around the world.

Were you supportive?

How did you offer reassurances to employees you relied on to manage the front lines and keep your business afloat?

Did you listen to your employees? Likewise, there are logistics to deal with for those employees who work from home.

Work will never be the same.

How does management deal with this type of situation? Not only do you have people to pay but you need to make sure you remain sustainable.

Some companies have had to do the worst, just let go of their employees.

Other companies had better options, such as two weeks' pay and then a furlough until their job returns.

We have been discussing the obvious need for lean inclusion. However, we can move beyond what we feel needs to be done for inclusion just by referencing examples of how certain businesses are measuring up in this area on their own.

These businesses we are highlighting offer us insights into how they are:

- Properly tackling the issues

- Where challenges in the gap between frontline workers and others exist

At this moment, more businesses fall into the latter category. This is what we are setting out to change. In all cases, through the case study examples, solutions can be discovered and implemented.

The topic of inclusion has never been more appropriate to discuss than during the COVID-19 outbreak. This virus has exposed the most vulnerable in the workplace.

Each of these case studies shows the problems that exist in systems where frontline workers' needs are not addressed.

Amazon

With most of the United States having been on lockdown for an extended period, businesses like Amazon boomed even more. The result of this was the need for more of the frontline workers (those in their warehouses) than previously, all to keep up with the high demand. Amazon's grocery service, in particular, has really been hit hard with a demand close to fifty times higher than usual. Add in the expectation that how we shop and entertain ourselves will be changed forevermore, and the importance of frontline workers is highlighted even more than it once was.

Amazon's biggest challenge is keeping enough employees to fill all the orders. These workers are the pulse of the entire Amazon empire and reliance on them is imperative to the company's success. This surge in orders tested Amazon's limit and changed the company relationship with the frontline employees. Through workplace organizational efforts, employees are now demanding:

- Better pay

- Better sick leave

- A cleaned and sanitized warehouse

- More of a voice in how the company is run

Employee protests erupted at many centers. Some people were even fired, forcing Amazon to respond. The company said no one was fired for speaking out about their workplace conditions, and those who were fired were let go because they had been on paid quarantine and violated safety measures by going to the on-site protest.

Today, Amazon has raised wages and added quarantine leave, while also offering overtime at double pay. They have also added safeguards in their factories such as tripling the janitorial staff and adding space between many of the workstations. Now they are auditing warehouses to ensure they are complying.

Corporate employees are also working from home, which is another factor to highlight the differences of frontline workers and those behind the scenes. Although unpaid, at first these necessary employees stayed home as the panic buying set in. This is when these workers were needed most. Consequently, loads of products were sent to warehouses from distributors, and they sat there because not enough workers were available to stock them. The point came when Amazon warehouses had to stop accepting new shipments unless they were priority items. Health care and baby supplies are two examples.

This demand does zero to keep people safe from the virus. Contractors can get the virus and if they go about their work, Amazon's frontline workers remain at risk. Some facilities had to close for deep cleaning after employees tested positive.

Employees eventually began to work staggered shifts so they were not too close to one another when they entered the facility. Some of the blowback included employee organizers stating that Amazon needed to prove they were an essential service.

The result for Amazon was a demand to value and protect its essential workers, who were most at-risk for many illnesses. COVID-19 just happened to be the one that brought the problem to the forefront (Weise & Conger, 2020).

Key Takeaway from this study

Businesses will struggle to remain vibrant when their frontline workers are at a health risk and no policies are in place to help negate this risk.

Costco

Costco's headquarters is in King County, Washington. This area was the epicenter of the first massive COVID-19 outbreak in the United States. The start of their challenges began in mid-March 2020 when employee Regina Lee took on an extra shift even though she was not feeling well. She passed away just a few days later, creating the first confirmed case of COVID-19 at Costco's headquarters. Her mother and sister died shortly thereafter.

As this was happening, work-from-home orders were being implemented and while many companies shifted to accommodate the policy, Costco did not. Its reason, according to CEO Craig Jelinek, was that it would not be fair to the "great number of Costco employees locally and across the country" in its stores who could not. "Our jobs here are to support our retail business, and we're not prepared at this point to have corporate employees work from home." (Sacks, 2020).

Key Takeaway

Corporations must find ways to balance competing dynamics—employee confidentiality versus employees' rights to health and information; or solidarity with frontline workers versus the health risks to office workers.

Starbucks

The problems at Starbucks were highlighted with sick employees working despite the warnings that were already present, as well as some workers being exposed through someone they loved. This is not different from the rest of the world's story, but how Starbucks chose to handle the crisis bears highlighting.

Here are two outcomes of Starbucks early-on actions:

- Unclear sick pay rules left many workers having to choose between working their shifts sick or staying home without pay

- The decisions due to major public health implications was put on the shoulders of the local branch managers

Eventually, two solutions were offered. First, they started to have drive-thru-only service, and second, they began to offer three days paid catastrophe leave to all employees. This sounded good, but it was a reactive response to an active situation. Extensive numbers of people had already been exposed.

Buzzfeed investigated this and the conclusion was that Starbucks, along with dozens of other companies, had kept stores open without any plan for how to operate during a pandemic. The result was that anxious hourly rate employees had to work without sufficient protocols to protect them (Samaha, 2020).

Measures have been put into place now but it does not change the fact that employee well-being in a massive crisis had no protocol in place. If there had been no pushback on a major level, would a specific policy even be in place?

Starbucks has many appealing qualities that its employees benefit from. A few examples are:

- Higher pay
- Better benefits than those offered by industry competitors
- Employees are called partners because they receive a share of the company upon hire
- Tuition assistance is available for employees

- An employee can apply for a hardship grant when facing financial strain

These benefits help to attract great talent, but they are not as effective if the company does not protect its team members during the worst of times. Employees recognize that protective policies are in place but question whether there would have been an adequate response to COVID-19 without outside pressure.

Key Takeaway

If your company strategy for incentivizing recruitment and retention of talent includes generous perks for employees, you must make sure that you are also taking care of the basics of making sure that they are protected.

The Educational Divide

Once again, coronavirus is paving the way for our world by pointing out ways in which we control the virus and expose weaknesses in our cultures. Call it the great divide, if you will. Education is one of these areas and the following is a broad sweep of how our world has changed, leaving a gap in education as a result.

People in rural areas are hindered from their students receiving a solid education because many of the areas lack adequate access to broadband. This hinders their ability to provide online learning as an option. It creates challenges with:

- Affordability to have a device that can support online learning management platforms

- Busy parents and guardians who cannot effectively facilitate online learning

In short, truly little was working as it should with the new online schooling system. Some children could not gain access to a phone that would work for classes. Many of these children have parents who are not willing to engage in the learning process with them, or to help fill in the gaps in this instant virtual world. Plus, the technology was not always reliable (Zhong, 2020).

These setbacks have led to a further divide in education. Some of it is affordability related but not all of it. Some parents simply do not take the initiative to invest in education. Some also do whatever they want, creating distractions that make learning difficult (noise in the background, for example).

As the pandemic drags on, there are growing concerns in areas of high poverty that students are being left behind. "We're not dealing with an affluent community in a private school, so the foundation wasn't laid over the last decade," Los Angeles Schools Superintendent Austin Beutner said when asked about technology's role in the pandemic.

He went on to add that 68 percent of the district's students were connected on any normal day before the pandemic. The cause for the change is a combination of a lack of resources that children have access to (reliable internet, for example) and different expectations depending on the parent's socioeconomic status.

With the risk of lower-income students not having access to adequate internet or even having a device that works properly, they are beginning to fall behind peers. And even with the cost of education being assessed per student, the challenges of getting reliable cable into rural areas is a problem.

It should be noted that reliable internet for all has been a concern long before the coronavirus. However, before it was recommended. Now, and perhaps forever, it is essential to close the gap of the educated and the struggling. These startling statistics show the importance of this:

- Pew found that the 'homework gap' -- the lack of a reliable Internet connection to do homework -- was more pronounced among Black, Hispanic and lower-income families. Even before the coronavirus pandemic, about 17 percent of teens between the ages of thirteen and seventeen said they were often (or sometimes) unable to finish homework assignments because of the lack of a connection or a computer.

- Michigan State University's Quello Center found that Michigan students without high-speed Internet access have lower overall grade point averages than their peers. They are less likely to spend time on homework; they perform worse on standardized tests; and are less likely to plan to attend college.

To counteract these abysmal statistics, some steps have been taken. While these steps help to alleviate the solution.

- Provisioning of mobile hotspots, either checked out from libraries or provided through programs

- Addition of Wi-Fi access on school buses

- A broadband stipend for homes

One heartbreaking statistic was noted by Superintendent Beutner. He indicated that "many of the 15,000 high school students who weren't initially connected also struggled with attendance even in ordinary times. Among them are the students living in the deepest poverty or the foster care system. Roughly 70,000 students in LAUSD (Los

Angeles Unified School District) are experiencing some form of homelessness." This is perhaps the most disheartening because a child who experiences homelessness has a significantly lower chance of growing up with the full support and education they deserve (Reston, 2020)..

New York City made a plan to offer 300,000 internet-enabled iPads to students who had no access to technology for their classes. Key takeaways:

- Students who are not effectively educated have a lower chance of breaking the cycle of poverty that they may be experiencing. The gaps in education during the pandemic only exacerbated this dynamic.

- Technology based businesses are starting to step in and help to fill the gap between children and technology.

- We live in a world where access to technology and online resources are mandatory for long term success, and this means we need to ensure it is accessible to all.

Verizon Wireless

With a goal to cultivate more women leaders, preferably from within its own ranks, Verizon Wireless had a choice to make. One that came with the need for action. Part of its credo states: "We embrace diversity and personal development not only because it's the right thing to do, but also because it's smart business." Still, they struggled with recruiting and retaining women.

It should be noted that a study of 353 companies in the Fortune 500 found that those with the most women in senior management are over 30 percent more profitable than the rest. Verizon is a company with a strong focus on equality in this area, both because it's the right thing to do and because they strive to be a profitable enterprise.

This initiative began with a partnership with PRISM International and its Women's Leadership Forum: Women at Work: Being an Advocate for Your Own Success, a program made available to hundreds of women across the enterprise. It is a fast-paced and highly interactive program to help women explore situations they face in today's workplace, while also encouraging them to reach higher levels of personal effectiveness. The goal is precise: explore strategies and tips for continued professional growth and development. Verizon's stated desire is to:

- Understand why women leaders are imperative to a company's success

- Find strategies for success in challenging times in today's workplace

- Explore ways to build a career that is in alignment with personal value and leveraging your differences

- Share conditions of retention

These conferences have led to continued engagement with women who are employed by Verizon. According to one of Verizon's regional vice presidents, "For every year that there was a women's conference on the West Coast, the women that I spoke with are still motivated, engaged, inspired and empowered. They still speak of the great experience they had at the conference and often cite their own personal success stories regarding what they used from the conference."

Other conference participants included their testimonials:

- "You have no idea how your message is touching people, I am only a project lead right now, but after your speech today I realize the impact I can have and I am going to apply for a promotion."

- "I had no idea how empowering this would be -I have so many ideas I am going to take back to my call center. I am excited to start my folks down a new path that can help everyone."

- "I have been to one of your previous sessions. I was recently transferred and I was able to use the skills you taught last time to make a transition. The men I work with have no idea what I am going to bring back to them this time!"

These initiatives have shown results. Verizon ranked high on DiversityInc's Top 50 List for its efforts to recruit, retain, and promote women. Its inclusive talent development best practices for minorities was also a factor in this ranking. It has also been named as a Top Organization for Multicultural Business Opportunities, an honor given through votes cast by minority and women-owned suppliers (PRISM International, 2013).

Key Takeaway

Consider the time and attention you invest in your inclusion initiatives as seeds. Once initially cultivated, those seeds will bear fruit that will create its own seeds. Employees who feel respected, valued, and supported will engage others and that will bear its own positive fruit.

Barilla

Barilla is an Italian company which had no formal practice of addressing diversity and inclusion back in 2013. It took one incident to change this: the company's chairman told someone that they could not feature advertisements with same-sex couples.

After this, there was a backlash, one that the existing executives decided to tackle head-on and not explain away. The company's general counsel Talita Erickson was asked to become its first chief diversity officer. With this came a great deal of change to the diversity and inclusion culture.

The appointment coincided with a seminal moment in the company's history: the launch of its inaugural Diversity and Inclusion Board, consisting of ten senior-level employees and a separate external advisory board, which includes three high-profile public figures, including a civil rights activist, a paralympic champion, and an esteemed academic leader.

"It was important for us to garner different perspectives," reflects Erickson, "so we sought out external expertise, and we're very fortunate to be collaborating with three highly respected figures."

In order to start making the changes they wished to experience, an assessment of the organization was done. The hope was to gain a precise understanding of skill gaps, workforce awareness, and also to build a strong business case for diversity and inclusion.

Then Barilla's top executives were interviewed to gain insight into their company culture as it relates to diversity, equity, and inclusion. They did this with all eight countries they operate facilities in, making it a global initiative, hosting meetings in the countries' native tongues to ensure authentic, clear, and honest communication took place.

Data was collected and a plan was put into place.

By 2014, the initiative was rolled out, starting with office employees, followed by sales and plant teams over the next two years. The program covered topics such as awareness of unconscious biases and the need to develop cross-cultural agility. They strived to cover the full gamut of diversity and inclusion, as well as the necessity for empathy in the workplace culture.

The goal of the diversity and inclusion initiative was to intertwine business strategy and growing profitability. This included daily activities, as well as cultural differences in how food is prepared and consumed around the world.

When put into action, Barilla's results speak for themselves.

- Barilla received a perfect score in the Human Rights Campaign Corporate Equality Index every year since its first perfect score in 2014.

- In 2015, Barilla's CEO, Claudio Colzani, was invited to sign the UN Women's Empowerment Principles.

- The company has supported the launch of two Employee Resource Groups: "Voce" for LGBT-QIA+ employees and allies, and "Balance" to help advance gender balance.

- HR continuously monitors and intervenes on key related people metrics, being accountable for reducing bias in talent management

With each year, the commitment continues from Barilla. Their goal is a perfect scorecard in this area (Tapia, 2019).

Key Takeaway

Once a culture is identified that does not practice diversity and inclusion, company leaders have a choice to move forward with inclusion or else to face the backlash of its exclusion.

Accenture

Accenture has been ranked #1 in the Thomson Reuters Diversity and Inclusion Index, which shows it takes diversity and inclusion seriously. All the employees at the company are required to create and sustain an inclusive environment, with its website even stating: "No one should be discriminated against because of their differences, such as age, ability, ethnicity, gender, gender identity and expression, religion or sexual orientation. Our rich diversity makes us more innovative and more creative, which helps us better serve our clients and our communities."

This result has not just happened without concrete steps being taken and embraced by all the Accenture staff. The firm's hope is that it will be gender neutral by 2025 with their 50-by-25 initiative. This goal is centered on reaching 50 percent female employment by 2025. In order to achieve this goal, the business has taken steps to attract, retain, advance, and sponsor women on their path to achieving a gender-balanced workforce.

These steps include:

- Launching initiatives that provide women employees with skills and place high-performing women in fast-track programs

- Collaborating across business and government to promote gender equality in the workplace, with commitments and pledge programs that include the White House Equal Pay Pledge, Paradigm for Parity, and Catalyst CEO Champions for Change—each of these promoting collaborative efforts toward a gender-balanced workforce.

Another distinction for Accenture is that it actively hires and works toward retention and inclusion of people with disabilities. All employees are trained to fully interact with technology, regardless of functional disabilities. "They also are empowering persons with disabilities every day through their Global Persons with Disabilities Champions Network, which organizes local networking, collaboration, mentoring and awareness-building activities for persons with disabilities—as well as caregivers and colleagues—throughout the year."

Also, with Accenture's belief that diversity leads to innovativeness, the company provides an inclusive environment for all employees, regardless of sexual orientation, gender identity, or expression. These objectives are achieved through:

- Recruitment

- Retention and promotion

- Professional development programs

- Equal pay and benefits

These steps, along with continued focus on being a front-runner in the diversity and inclusion space, are continually nurtured through cultural competence to create an environment of inclusion. Accenture sees this as its competitive advantage and feels diversity will become a bottom-line contributor (*Case Studies - Companies That Are Changing the Equation with Diversity and Inclusion*, 2019) .

Key Takeaway

The initiatives that grow a business to its best potential are ones that are inclusive of new ideas, all types of people, and a common goal for success.

Arabella Advisors

Even in the philanthropic sector there is a great need for diversity and inclusion. They are essential to any social mission. The D5 Coalition, a five-year initiative to advance diversity and inclusion in philanthropy, offers an example of how this desire played out for it. As part of its work, the coalition set out to identify the most progressive diversity and inclusion policies, practices, and the roadblocks to effective program initiatives within philanthropic organizations.

A few of its findings were:

- People of color are still underrepresented at foundation leadership levels

- A lack of reliable data about the number of women, people of color, LGBT people, and people with disabilities in decision-making positions within foundations presents an ongoing challenge

D5 Director Kelly Brown stated, "The data itself may not be telling the whole story because many foundations have yet to share information about personnel and grant making." And the organizations they work with to share the success of the diversity and inclusion aspirations tell a revealing story.

Arabella Advisors is an organization that advises foundations and donors on philanthropic strategy. It was growing rapidly, especially at junior and mid-level staff. Because of all this rapid change, Arabella felt disconnected from those it served. At the same time, those it served were placing a bigger emphasis on diversity and inclusion.

To tackle the situation, the senior leadership set up some committees that made inclusion goals but it was hard to get upper management to accept accountability for the goals, as the goals were not fully understood. This limited their ability to become truly inclusive.

A few of the advancements senior leadership made included:

- Broader recruiting networks and relationships with professional associations whose members brought new experiences to the firm

- Seeking out more "diversity candidates"

These were good initiatives but lacked the important training on how to implement the recommendations.

After two years, the leadership team had to take a step back and acknowledge that they had misjudged how to be a diverse and inclusive firm.

Then Arabella Advisors decided to approach diversity, equity, and inclusion in a similar manner as other firm-wide strategic issues. They designated people to lead the charge and be accountable, integrating it into the broader goals and infrastructure, and identifying outsiders to fill the gaps in expertise.

Other notable steps included:

- A brand-new HR department took responsibility for the firm's commitment to diversity and set a simple goal for the first year: to develop a long-term vision and strategy for what a diverse, equitable, and inclusive Arabella should look like.

- The team reached out to diversity experts and external groups with diversity, equity, and inclusion success stories, to gain understanding that diversity goes beyond demographics and statistics. It is woven into the fabric of the workplace, from recruiting to casual activities such as work happy hours.

- The team asked staff members about diversity and how they supported it. This was done through surveys and interviews.

- Arabella began tracking demographic data in a systematic way, which highlighted the extent to which racial and ethnic minorities were underrepresented at the firm.

- The organization eliminated some of its outdated practices, such as only promoting dominant and extroverted personalities, and not listening to the voices of those with other personalities.

It was through seeking outside perspectives that Arabella achieved clarity on how to become more diverse, inclusive, and equitable. The leadership team ultimately discovered that every aspect of their systems, processes, and culture fed into how diverse, equitable, and inclusive they were.

To further address their challenges, Arabella Advisors took several steps. Here are some of the biggest highlights.

- They set a goal of increasing the racial and ethnic diversity of the firm so that it better reflected the general population. A revamped recruiting team identified and cultivated partnerships with organizations that would connect us with candidates from a broader set of backgrounds.

- A partnership with the DC chapter of the National Black MBA Association was forged. Arabella and the DC chapter co-hosted member meetings and events.

- The organization affirmed their commitment to diversity, equity, and inclusion in their branding and with their recruiting materials.

- They trained hiring managers to understand unconscious bias and its impact on candidate pools.

- The leadership team disallowed the rejection of potential employees based on a hiring team's claim that the candidate was not a "cultural fit."

- All staff received an intensive, full-day training about what constituted an equitable and inclusive environment.

- They brought on inclusion leaders. These leaders were tasked with working on an ongoing basis with leadership, HR, and key staff to shift the internal culture, processes, and models to better integrate these values.

These more definitive actions led to better results. For example, in 2015, the racial and ethnic diversity of the firm increased by 32 percent. They were also able to identify many ways in which the staff felt disconnected and use inclusion leaders to help develop a multipronged strategy to incorporate diversity, equity, and inclusion into the firm's culture, recruiting and hiring, and client relationships.

All these initiatives took commitment and dedication to implement them so they became part of the natural culture of Arabella Advisors. Facing the failures and challenges allowed Arabella to experience the successes of a diverse culture (Ganguli & Murphy, 2019).

Key Takeaway

The process of developing inclusion and diversity is one that is not instantaneous. It takes a commitment and desire to create a new and inclusive culture where people come together.

BLUEPRINTS FOR CHANGE

There is hope and perhaps even a blueprint for change that is offered through organizations that have embraced why the workplace needs to be shifted. This offers a bright spot in the pandemic that has changed all our lives.

Some businesses evolved through the pandemic, which led to new practices that are the way work needs to be done in the future. According to the article, Evolving COVID-19 Responses of World's Largest Companies, which was featured on Gallup's website, three benefits have emerged (Emond & Maese, 2021):

- Leaders are adding new means of supporting employees

- COVID-19 has created a whole new paradigm for human resource allocation

- Leaders are focused on current and future needs

Some of the protocols that have emerged as a result of the pandemic are below.

- Tracing the contacts of employees who have tested positive

- Using corporate social responsibility funds, employee relief funds, and industry or foundation funds to aid employees diagnosed with COVID-19 or those who have family members diagnosed with COVID-19

- Adding new benefits for all employees, such as childcare subsidies and reimbursement

- Adding benefits (e.g., paid time off, health insurance extensions) for part-time or hourly workers who previously didn't have them

- Offering reimbursement for costs/premiums related to COVID-19 that aren't covered by insurance, such as tests, doctor visits or hospitalization

- Employee-crowdsourced assistance, such as babysitting

- Equipment, operating systems–such as staggered shifts–and physical barriers that separate employees from each other and customers

Companies have had to make some hard choices to increase their chances of staying in business. Businesses that are struggling have had to employ some of the following strategies:

- Reduce hours or create job-shares to preserve as many employees as possible

- Reduce pay by, on average, 10 percent to 50 percent

- Place employees on furlough

- Institute internal labor arbitrage

- Freeze hiring or hire only for critical roles

- Rescind job offers

- Cancel internships

- Cancel contracts

- Issue layoffs, though many intend to rehire if possible

- Provide benefits to employees on furlough

- Provide full severance to laid-off workers, with some extending the post-exit benefit period and some staggering payments

- Incentivize early retirement among high earners

- Assist laid-off employees in accessing unemployment benefits

The innovative change route is the route of the future if you have an interest in receiving positive attention about your company's efforts for diversity and inclusion.

Josh Bersin, who writes about business trends and human resources, shared insights into the advantages businesses have today when it comes to creating stronger diversity and inclusion. In his article, "COVID-19 May Be The Best Thing That Ever Happened To Employee Engagement," talks about how the pandemic has been a catalyst for transformation for business (Bersin, 2020).

Employees are being treated better than ever, which means employee engagement is going up.

It seems that businesses are bending over backwards to maintain happier employees. They may not want to, necessarily, but they are being forced to do so. And despite themselves, they are improving their work cultures substantially. Here are five areas of change:

1. Businesses are protecting their workers. "It's clear from our data that the #1 thing on the minds of most employees today is personal financial security. Yes, they're worried about their health, but above that they're worried about their jobs, the viability of the company, and their ability to take care of their children,

families, and parents. And for millennials and younger workers, they are now worried about their careers.

2. We are seeing an increased focus on personal productivity, well-being, and personal resilience. "As more than 90 percent of companies started their work-at-home program, the first issue they deal with is getting computers, internet access, security, and tools into people's homes." This wasn't easy but was managed through offering things like a Remote Work Bootcamp to help employees get into the swing of their new way to work.

3. There has been a huge transformation in learning, especially for leaders. "While most companies have shut down face-to-face training, the consumption of online learning is skyrocketing. People are home and they want to learn about the crisis, their jobs, and what they can do to stay ahead."

4. A new and improved leadership culture has emerged. "A Willis Towers Watson study shows that 63 percent of HR professionals believe their organizational culture has improved, 59 percent believe their employee well-being has improved, and 55 percent believe their employee experience has improved."

5. The order to "work at home" is working quite well. "The Willis study found that 79 percent of companies see a positive or neutral change in employee productivity, and only 21 percent said it went down. In other

words, remote work was ALWAYS a good idea, and now it's here to stay."

The results have been favorable including:

- Companies are building new programs in days instead of months, and two-thirds of respondents told us that they are *prioritizing relationships* like never before.

- Trust in business leaders has gone up. Ninety-five percent of the respondents in the Willis Towers Watson survey believe senior leaders have demonstrated a sincere interest in employee well-being, and *85 percent believe employees have trust and confidence in the job being done by senior execs.*

- Teams are coming together to listen to their people, talk, and work together on projects like never before. People are helping each other, asking each other how they're doing, and listening more than ever.

THE OPPORTUNITY

The coronavirus pandemic resulted in hundreds of thousands of deaths. The loss to the families is incalculable. The global economy will never completely recover. There has been a fundamental shift. But the opportunity of the shift is to rebuild a better future, to alter our trajectory onto a sustainable path. We are all now at a place where we are required to grow stronger and better together.

In this chapter we were able to:

- Learn through the experiences of Uber and Pepsi. Both these businesses would have benefited from their obvious errors if they had taken into account the importance of diversity and inclusion to their livelihoods.

- Goldman Sachs has potentially set a minimum requirement for companies that are going through the initial public offering process. While there are clearly greater opportunities to create equity, having this policy in place is an important step forward.

- Through understanding the five main business needs, we can:

  ‣ Have the best talent in our organizations

  ‣ Become more innovative in our products and services

  ‣ Gain understanding of the diversity that leads to our success

  ‣ Become a more profitable organization

  ‣ Put operating procedures and policies into place that protect all workers equally

  ‣ Come up with a stronger plan that takes the crisis out of any future pandemic-type situations a business could face.

From each case study we have gone through, we have taken away valuable lessons for you to learn from. We better understand:

- How some of the world's most notable businesses handled the COVID-19 pandemic. Some of these businesses have faced backlash for being unprepared to protect their frontline workers during this situation but are also credited with striving to bring balance to the situation through better choices.

- How the educational systems that are in place for much of our country fall short of meeting the needs of all their students. This especially pertains to underserved students and their ability to participate in the modern era with technology. By getting all students access to technology, they have a way to learn, grow, and become technology leaders of the future.

- That there are some success stories out there, such as what takes place at Verizon Wireless to advance women in the workplace.

- That a great lesson has been given to us through companies such as Arabella and Barilla. They have taught us that when solid diversity and inclusion initiatives are thought of, thought through, and implemented they do make a difference. This is also the only way that a company that developed a reputation for not inviting diversity and inclusion can change its course of action and make a difference.

- That some businesses have strengthened their work culture through the COVID-19 pandemic. They now serve as models for change other companies can base their operations off to find success. This was done through respect for all workers' health and well-being, combined with benefits and incentives to bring their employees peace of mind. When a business has its employees' backs, the employees are likely to return the favor and serve the business's best interests in return.

WELCOME TO THE MOVEMENT

We are writing this book as the world is recovering from being knocked on its ass.

People are being vaccinated. US leadership is changing. The reverberating echoes from the protests of the summer are fading, but not yet forgotten. The passion of protest can now give way to something more sustainable, more enduring.

The time is right for the moment to evolve into a movement.

This movement will require us to do more. It will require us to be more. These personal evolutions are critical to the greater cause. Cynicism has no place in who we must now be. Incrementalism doesn't belong there either. We must push past comfort to commitment. And we must do so as innovators. As people who know how to execute and not just pontificate on the process.

There is a danger in this moment. Many organizations will fall prey to it. Diversity and inclusion as performance is a real threat because it is the path of least resistance in the short term. It is action without progress. The inequities that 2020 exposed and amplified have sped up the process of change. The status quo of power being held almost exclusively by a single group is not sustainable in the long term. Equity is the equilibrium that all companies will move toward. It will happen because we, the people, will demand it. We will demand it with our voices and our money. Some of us will be forced to demand it with our lives. But the movement toward equity will happen. It means that power that is held will have to be released. This power shift is inevitable, driven by demographics and market forces. The question is how will you manage this shift. How will you engage with the movement?

The first part of this book gave you the context for this moment. We hope the information was fuel, that you used it to feed your mind and soul to execute. You will need to do the real work of this moment. You will need to be the movement toward a more equitable state. We can guarantee that this will be tough, tough work.

The next part of this book is a blueprint for movement. But don't get it confused. We don't presume to provide an answer for The Movement. That's a bigger thing and our work is a small part of the greater whole. We want to guide you toward movement, toward creating inclusion and equity in your organization. We will be with you all the way. We stand shoulder to shoulder with you, not just in this moment, but in the days, months, and years to come. We intend to teach, but also to learn. We hope to work with you. We want to gather best practices and share them with others who share our commitment.

Know this, your work will cost you something. It can and will deplete you. As Frederick Douglass noted, there is no progress without struggle, and power concedes nothing without a demand. So part of this work is ensuring that you refill your reserves. The last chapter of this book covers this topic. It is easy to overlook self-care as you do your work, but self-care is the foundation of self-preservation. It is required because inclusion work is long-term. It requires stamina and faith.

Welcome to the movement.

CHAPTER FIVE

HOW TO ASSESS YOUR CURRENT STATE

Remember Kelly, the chief diversity officer for ABC Corp. from Chapter One? Her company, a midsize Midwest manufacturing firm, was facing some real issues. After some investigation, she found that the company culture was a real liability. This was based on the fact that ABC Corp.'s track record on inclusion was abysmal. You may remember that one of Kelly's first steps to assess the current state of her company was to gather quantitative and qualitative data from a wide range of team members. What Kelly did was conduct a cultural audit.

A cultural audit is a powerful tool to assess the health of a company culture with real world, data-driven snapshots.

As an anthropologist, I believe that cultural audits are one of the most useful kinds of applied research, because they both uncover issues and provide a platform for people who do not always have a say in the way things are done at a company to be heard. Including their voices often yields direct value because they may have unique insight about processes, customers, or underlying issues.

When we conduct a cultural audit, we speak with management to get some context on the issues that catalyzed the audit. We develop a list of areas we want to initially explore within the company. Then we develop interview protocols to uncover insights. We conduct interviews, trying to create a baseline of the environment and dig into some of the dynamics that occur beneath the surface activity.

Based on the initial insights, we develop and administer surveys to employees, paying attention to how responses differ for specific groups including senior leadership, frontline workers, and direct reports of specific staff. We follow up the initial research with follow-up interviews and surveys to clarify points and measure change over time.

Understanding the difference over time is useful, especially if you are measuring the change in culture before and after a key event, such as a merger, the separation of a problem employee, or an initial public offering. Even without a specific milestone event, monitoring company culture over time is a wise investment, especially given its role in employee retention, customer satisfaction, and overall performance. Cultural audits play a key role in helping to assess how inclusive your organization feels to your team.

THE FOUR CATEGORIES OF BUSINESS

So you've done your cultural audit. What is the next step? Well, it is likely that you will find your organization is in one of four categories as it relates to inclusion. Here, we use the metaphor of a house being on fire to underscore the urgency of the situation. The categories are as follows.

Category One: Your house is on fire right now.

What it looks like: You are facing an immediate crisis in which team members do not feel supported, valued or respected. You need a mitigating strategy right now. The situation is either currently out of control or it will be soon. The issues may be subject to public scrutiny via social or traditional media. There is likely already some chatter about these issues on internal social media and/or communication channels.

Potential underlying issues: Lack of diversity; significant and visible inequity based on race or gender; significant but less visible inequity based on age, ability, and/or socioeconomic background; patterns of behavior consistent with discrimination; no clear commitment to inclusion.

Category Two: Your house has a potential gas leak.

What it looks like: There are persistent problems that occasionally surface, but they have not yet flared up to become a major issue. However, if the data from your cultural audit were analyzed, systemic issues would surface.

Potential underlying issues: Lack of diversity; evidence of inequity based on race and gender; significant but less visible inequity based on age, ability, and/or socioeconomic background; patterns of behavior consistent with discrimination; superficial or performative commitment to inclusion

Category Three: Your house has burned down.

What it looks like: Your toxic culture has created an unsustainable workplace that is winding down, suffocating it to a slow death. Major issues have been exposed and the negative legal, financial, and marketplace consequences are insurmountable and inevitable.

Potential underlying issues: Lack of diversity; significant and visible inequity based on race, gender, age, ability, and/or socioeconomic background; patterns of behavior consistent with discrimination; disdain for inclusion-related efforts from leaders and/or other internal influencers

Category Four: Your house is in order.

What it looks like: You have an inclusive and sustainable culture in which employees, customers, and stakeholders feel supported, valued, and respected.

Potential underlying issues: Ongoing monitoring and maintenance of inclusive culture is a practice that management has invested in and is committed to. Commitment to inclusion is clear and supported by the vast majority of team members in such a way that it attracts employees to the organization.

Today, most businesses fall into the first two categories, and a few have regretfully moved to the third category. We hope that someday, most successful businesses will be in Category Four—they have their house in order.

However you might categorize your organization, it is important that you take some specific actions to move toward a healthy inclusive culture. It is here where we diverge with more conventional approaches toward inclusion. There are dozens of templates for self assessments on offer on the internet and through diversity consultants. We believe that your inclusion assessment should be customized for your organization. We believe that the objectives and key results you create must be closely tied to your specific organizational goals. You cannot effectively manage inclusion with a one-off framework that has no meaningful connection to your overall organizational planning. To do so is to make your diversity, equity, and inclusion efforts less relevant. It also hinders accountability because performance metrics typically drive advancement and pay. Creating a separate inclusion initiative will make it difficult to properly incent your team to contribute meaningfully.

You should also make sure that the tools you use to monitor your progress reside in the same place that other performance metrics reside. Organization-wide visibility of diversity and inclusion metrics brings accountability and sends a clear message about their importance.

So ultimately, how do you assess inclusion for your organization? Well, it depends. If you have a formal strategic planning process, then your inclusion efforts are simply a part of that process. If your organizational planning is less formal, then you may adopt a more informal approach. However, you still need the basics of creating a baseline, objective-setting, measurement, and maintenance.

Creating a framework for assessing your organizational inclusion efforts is only part of what needs to be done. The day-to-day management of your organization and your team is what creates the experience of inclusion or exclusion for the people inside of an organization. And it's more challenging than it has ever been to implement the best practices of diversity and inclusion. The COVID-19 pandemic and racial reckoning have put inequity on the forefront of popular conversation. The impact encompasses and overlaps our home and work lives. What is most important is that we make sure that we take care of each other and ourselves. Below are several issues to monitor for our peers, our direct reports, and our managers that have added an unfamiliar level of complexity to being effective leaders.

UNDERSTANDING THE MANAGEMENT ISSUES

There are several management issues that directly connect with enabling inclusion and belonging in the workplace that have emerged as our world shifted in 2020. Let's examine each below.

They are:

- Working from home

- The digital divide

- Parental status

- Mental health

- Physical health

Work from Home

The "luxury" of working from home does not come without hassles. One of the primary issues is the ability to recognize how people experience the crisis and the option differently based on the kind of jobs they have. There are clear differences on what people's home life looks like and what they have to take care of in their home that is nonwork related.

Consider these questions:

- Who is in their current household?

- Is there embarrassment about where they live?

- Does the team member have a private space to work?

- Is there a lack of technology causing a digital divide?

Knowing how to address these real-life concerns is paramount to successfully navigating a rewarding direction for the at-home worker.

It also demands paying attention to the other side of the equation—the frontline worker who has to go to the office.

Issues will arise from those businesses which have both frontline workers on an hourly salary and nonessential workers who can attempt to work from home. Both sides deserve attention so inclusivity is demonstrated on a corporate level.

For example, if a company institutes a policy of flexible work hours for at-home workers, this is not going to apply to frontline workers. This creates a situation where rules are being unevenly applied. The frontline workers are the ones keeping the company afloat. How do we manage this situation and not slight people in the process?

Those who manage teams have to increase their sensitivity to the people on their teams. Below are a few suggestions that will help

- **Know who has family around and who does not**: People working from home may be in isolation during the process, due to either age or living alone. This adds an extra dimension of challenges to dealing with the pandemic.

- **Ask how people are doing:** Engaging in a genuine conversation and being authentically concerned about another's well-being is not only good courtesy but also good for building team cohesiveness.

In general, people are more on edge than they were pre-COVID. Their needs are greater because of the uncertainty. And we're not just managers and employees, we are humans. This needs to be processed, and there is no "water cooler" at work to do this around; this is problematic.

The Digital Divide

Associated with the at-home worker is the technology to attend virtual meetings and perform the job as effectively as it could be done in the office.

If you have a meeting with, say, twenty people and you agree to connect via Zoom, it is only effective if everyone knows how to use this platform. And if one of the members, especially a leader, does not, there is going to be a massive curve of adoption that impacts everyone. You need time to figure it out.

To have prepared employees, this means you need to take into account:

- Learn a platform

- Navigate between platforms

- Get past the hiccups of cameras and technology

This is new for some folks. Prior to having to, they never had a desire to gain an aptitude in these areas. This means these are the people who can fall through the cracks. Now, everyone needs to know how to navigate calls and technology. This know-how is now a factor that impacts inclusion.

This means they also need:

- The proper hardware

- Software for programs

Getting people to the stage of digital literacy and fluency is important. And this engagement needs to be done in a significant way so no one is left behind or unprepared.

Much of this is exacerbated by the environment and conditions of the worker. Back in the day, CEOs had secretaries print off emails. They had to take a big leap forward to get to the point of checking their email for themselves. It was a technological advancement for them.

In the present day, learning email seems like a minor step, doesn't it? There is so much catch-up on the horizon for many people.

Parental Status

Everyone is going to have a different experience when they work from home. Part of this will have to do with their environment. Which environment are they in?

- One where their workflow is uninterrupted because a spouse can take care of the children.

- One where there is always activity in the background (e.g. children running around)

Privilege during pandemic and crisis is not universal. Take the story of a former colleague. At the outset of COVID, he would have breakfast with his family, then head off to his office located in a separate area of the house to work. At lunch, he'd go in to enjoy it with his family, and then back to work until the day was done. What a nice routine, ideal by many people's standards. He was fortunate, well-fed and supported by a wife to take care of the kids and other aspects of the house.

What about people not so fortunate?

They may experience these types of issues:

- Being unable to return calls to colleagues because they are helping their children with homework

- Being constantly distracted by their environment

If you were the sole adult in your household, would you know how to balance your work and your children's school work effectively?

Could you make it so you were working later in the evening and getting up earlier to do your work so your children stayed on a good schedule?

And even if you could do that, would it be acceptable to your coworkers to receive responses from you at these obscure hours only?

It is not an easy task to raise children and earn a living from home, simultaneously. This is exactly what we were thrown into by the pandemic.

This stress and potential for problems remain key lessons. In crisis:

- Workers experience stress when they feel their children don't understand why they are not focused on their needs.

- Workers also experience stress when they feel their coworkers are slighted because of the attention they give their children during work hours.

These are real issues that still need real solutions.

We also need to address caretakers of parents. How do you manage their needs while juggling your own? These are the kinds of real struggles that workers carry and are not easily addressed and resolved.

Mental Health

More than ever before, life's uncertainties have made it necessary for employers to offer mental health services to their employees.

At an alarming rate, people are identifying the need for mental health and wellness care. Talking openly about mental health issues is important and a proactive way to keep our eyes on the rise. Furthermore, people who you may not expect to have these types of challenges are bravely coming forth and admitting they are struggling. This is a byproduct of uncertain times.

Add in the loneliness and isolation for some people and it presents challenges. For others, they are using this time for self-reflection and improvement. Either way, responses cannot be assumed, which means services should be provided. Every employee should have access to something if it is needed, even with many businesses's wallets tightening.

A furloughed worker should be able to have the benefit of mental health care to help them through challenges in their lives.

A frontline worker should have an outlet to deal with stress they may fall under because they are worried about carrying COVID-19 home to their family.

Physical Health

We will never go back to the way things were, which is actually great for advancement of stronger, more universally accepted diversity and inclusion in the workplace. Part of this will entail realizing that our health will never be viewed in the same way again, either.

One of the biggest challenges frontline workers will have in the future is their response if someone should cough. They may not want to be near them, especially if they have never had COVID-19 at that time. Right now, having a tickle in your throat when you are in public can lead to intense scrutiny from others.

THE NEW RULES

How many rules have been rewritten because of COVID? We can think of these (and the list keeps growing):

- Customer experiences

- How people think about businesses

- The job you have

- The manner in which people conduct their business

This new tone will require us all to adjust and many of us may find it to be quite uncomfortable. That's okay. Change, by its nature, is uncomfortable at first. It'll be interesting to see how many people change professions after the pandemic—whether by choice or force. Not all positions will feel necessary or critical to an operation's success.

Add in the fact that some people will be gun shy about hiring and about taking risks.

This is why it is more important than it previously was to have savings to carry you through when money falls short. This is one of the things an hourly rate worker is least likely to have. Every penny they make is accounted for. So how do you deal with that? Financial literacy classes can help but they are not an end-all solution.

For those who find themselves in the situation of having to apply for unemployment, they are facing obstacles. These include:

- Navigating the way to do this online, as most of these offices are closed. If they don't have a computer where do they go to do this? If they don't know how to use a computer, who can they rely on to teach them or do the paperwork for them?

- Not knowing how to do an online search. Not everyone is online every day and knows how to find information on the web.

These habits we have developed over our lifetimes need to be adjusted. Which serve us still and which do not? If it doesn't serve you, you'd best strive to change it.

Which habits serve me and which habits don't? In this new age of awareness of our mortality, we'd best all find out.

Life will continue on, with or without us. The circle of life happens whether we want it to or not. Getting to a better place where you can help a person while you are here will matter.

There is no room for a pity party any longer. You can take solace in the few things that have not changed for anyone, which are:

- The need to be valued

- The need to be respected

Now that the house has burned down and inequities are brought to life, what do we do in the aftermath? Engagement in our workplace and community is what will heal us and generate positive changes for a more inclusive, equalized world. That engagement ought to be diverse and inclusive if it has any chance of being meaningful and impactful in the future.

THE OPPORTUNITY

With a clearer idea of what our biggest challenges are to overcome the great divide that currently exists in the workplace and parts of society, we are preparing ourselves to act accordingly.

- We are committed to becoming better equipped to manage the pressing and important issues that are now a part of our workplace. These include:
  - Working at home, which comes with both benefits and challenges
  - Closing the digital divide that stops us from performing our work to the best of our abilities
  - Learning how to be teachers to our children while also being responsible to our work obligations
  - Taking care of our parents whose need for our help has not been altered by the onset of the COVID-19 pandemic

- ‣ Making sure our mental health is tended to during these times of stress and crisis (knowing this is critical to our ability to manage all that is being tossed our direction)

- ‣ Being mindful of our physical health by trying to prevent illnesses or passing them along to others, including your family

- Now we are creating new rules of engagement that have the potential to lead to a more unified future. This is being done by:

  - ‣ Having the awkward conversations

  - ‣ Investing in diversity and inclusion to leverage the workforce between serving interests of both essential and nonessential workers

  - ‣ Educating people on their need to have some financial security to get them through tough times

  - ‣ Creating a stronger, stand-up workforce that is valued and respected

  - ‣ Giving back to our communities and realizing our strength comes from all of us being strong, not just a select few

HOW TO MAKE CHANGE

Here is where the rubber meets the road. Here is where we talk about change.

This is the moment. It's clear that there is a problem. Now is the time to live up to the potential to make real, lasting change.

Let's get specific. In this chapter, we are going to focus on how to make change in the world of technology. Much of what we will talk about is applicable in other realms, but the tech space is one we know well. High-growth technology firms are also key drivers of job creation and opportunity. There is also a lot of opportunity for much higher levels of diversity, not to mention inclusion and equity.

Tech companies are challenging places to have conversations about inclusion, because many in this space are convinced that they are smarter and more accomplished than most. Those that are successful are also convinced that their own merits have been a key driver of that success. It is a domain that is also dominated by White men. One where women, Latinx, and Black people are truly in the minority, although diversity has improved since the early days of the internet.

Marlo's first company, jazzdigital Marketing, was a digital marketing firm that she founded with a small team in 1999. Among other things, they developed websites, created multimedia email campaigns, and created custom kiosk interfaces. Her clients included BMG Entertainment and Ford Motor Company. All of the founders were Black and based in Detroit. She remembers being at a trade show with her co-founders and an interactive kiosk that they designed. A group of White men were impressed with what we were doing, and asked us several times where the owners of the company were. "They thought we were joking when we indicated that the company was ours." Though decades have passed since that time, we still have not made the kind of progress in inclusion that the tech world itself has made. Tech founders who are not White males are underestimated and undercapitalized.

In 2018, only thirty-four Black female founders had ever raised $1 million in venture capital for their companies. As a cowriter and researcher of the first digitalundivided ProjectDiane report that released these findings, Marlo recognized the breadth of the gap. In 2018 alone, $131 billion across 8,949 deals was deployed, according to PitchBook and the National Venture Capital Association.

In 2020, that stat nearly tripled, with ninety-three Black women reporting they secured $1 million in investor backing for their businesses, according to the biennial ProjectDiane report.

Lack of equity in tech is no accident. The industry has long been the domain of White men touting proud stories of start-up adventures, with most of them missing diverse faces and plans of equitable inclusion.

Peter Thiel, founder of PayPal, returned to his alma mater Stanford in 2012 to teach his now famous "CS183: Start-ups" course. Thiel invited PayPal cofounder Max Levchin to guest lecture and asked Levchin, "How do you build culture?" Here is one of his more notable comments (Loder, 2019):

> The notion that diversity in an early team is important or good is completely wrong. You should try to make the early team as non-diverse as possible. There are a few reasons for this. The most salient is that, as a start-up, you're underfunded and undermanned. It is a big disadvantage, not only are you probably getting into trouble, but you don't even know what trouble that may be. Speed is your only weapon. All you have is speed.

He went on to share:

> PayPal once rejected a candidate who aced all the
> engineering tests because for fun, the guy said that
> he liked to play hoops. That single sentence lost him
> the job. No PayPal people would ever have used the
> word "hoops." Probably no one even knew how to
> play "hoops." Basketball would be bad enough. But
> "hoops?" That guy clearly wouldn't have fit in. He'd
> have had to explain to the team why he was going
> to go play hoops on a Thursday night. And no one
> would have understood him.

The culture for a start-up does need to be cohesive. Nobody
argues against this. The problem reveals itself when the cohesive culture becomes a culture of group think. There is a great
deal of research that indicates that diversity and inclusion,
when properly managed, have significant positive implications
on productivity. In the book, *The Diversity Bonus*, author Dr.
Scott Page discussed how cognitive diversity–often brought
to a team through identity diversity–reduces error rates and
increases innovation. Yet entrenched ideas of who makes the
best teams still persist. When it comes to women, Levchin had
this to say regarding a PayPal hiring decision:

> PayPal also had a hard time hiring women. An outsider
> might think that the PayPal guys bought into the stereo-
> type that women don't do CS [computer science]. But
> that's not at all true. The truth is that PayPal had trouble

hiring women because PayPal was just a bunch of nerds! They never talked to women. So how were they supposed to interact with and hire them?

One good hiring maxim is: whenever there's any doubt, there's no doubt, It's a good heuristic. More often than not, any doubt precluded a hire. But once this very impressive woman came to interview. There were some doubts, since she seemed reluctant to solve a coding problem. But her talk and demeanor—she insisted on being interviewed over a ping-pong game, for instance—indicated that she'd fit into the ubernerd, ubercoder culture. She turned out to be reasonably good at ping-pong. Doubts were suppressed. That was a mistake. She turned out to not know how to code. She was a competent manager but a cultural outsider. PayPal was a place where the younger engineers could and would sometimes wrestle with each other on the floor to solve disputes! If you didn't get the odd mix of nerdiness + alpha maleness, you just stuck out.

As you can imagine, Levchin's comments were met with a fair amount of debate from people with varying perspectives. Some agreed and some vehemently disagreed. In an effort to clear up what his true intentions were about this guest speaker spot in the classroom, he shared this perspective in a 2019 interview with Sequoia Capital.

In other companies that I've built or seen, there's the opposite. People are extremely well-liked across the teams—people loved each other as human beings—but they doubted the other person's competence... Anytime I've seen teams with these amazing love affairs, the cofounders cannot be separated, they're brothers and sisters together, you always want to probe: Do you really respect each other, or do you just really like each other? If your level of expertise isn't there and you're kind of making up for that by having a great relationship, it will not survive a single tough moment. In the middle of when everything is on the line—and we'll go back to loving each other, but right now, I just want you to not do your engineering job because you're not even that good of an engineer, even though you're the CTO—that's the end of the company. That will not survive.

The first statements are necessary in order to understand the importance of the last statement from Levchin. Clearly, the best results happen when you have the best talent at your company.

The best talent can come from a robust culture where the perspectives and input of different people make the company stronger. Everyone being like-minded or like-behaved is a weakness to the longevity of a business, regardless of the type of business it is.

Being intentional in your efforts is required and focusing on this aspect over system inertia is how you will build an "influencer framework" that leads to changes in a company's culture. The culture is a powerful force to be up against, as it requires individual desire to shift thinking, accept what may feel scary to a person in the old system, and realize that everyone will be best off with a policy, plan, and actions that embrace diversity and inclusion as assets to the organization.

REPORTING THE RESULTS

As one of the largest and most influential tech companies, Google is scrutinized, analyzed, and benchmarked. It is a leader that many companies follow. Every year Google releases a report about diversity and inclusion. Its 2019 findings are emblematic of the inclusion efforts for technology companies as a whole.

Here are a few of these statistics according to a *Forbes* article by Ruth Umoh (2020).

- There were modest gains in representation for women and people of color, and a disproportionately White, Asian, and male workforce.

- The percentage of Black hires in the U.S. grew from 4.8 percent in 2018 to 5.5 percent in 2019, a 0.7 percent increase.

- The percentage of Black hires in technical roles also grew by 0.7 percent.

- Latinx employees saw a dip in hiring, dropping from 6.8 percent in 2018 to 6.6 percent in 2019.

- The percentage of Latinx employees in technical roles increased by 0.2 percent.

- Female employees dropped from 33.2 percent of global hires in 2018 to 32.5 percent in 2019.

Women hired for technical positions remained at about 25.6 percent.

Overall, Google's workforce representation, including nontechnical roles, saw a slight uptick for most underrepresented groups with:

- Black and Latinx employees represented 9.6 percent of the US workforce in 2019.

- Women represented 32 percent of Google's global workforce, up from 31.6 percent in 2019.

Additionally, women and Latinx employees in leadership saw an increase of 0.6 percent and 0.4 percent respectively; however, the percentage of black employees in leadership positions didn't change and there was a slight drop >0.2 percent) of Native Americans in leadership roles.

Umoh goes on to state: "Although the needle has barely budged for women and people of color in tech over the last year, Google has made it a point to invest in diversity programs. Through its philanthropic arm, Google.org, the company committed $10 million to support low-income students and students of color in Bay Area STEM classrooms in 2019." This shows an initiative to train and educate a diverse group of people to be future leaders in industry, perhaps even theirs.

Furthermore, with the use of software such as a bias removal tool, there is an increase of 11 percent in applications from women. The company concedes it has much more to do and part of that includes retaining employees of underrepresented groups at their organization.

Google has made incremental investment in inclusion, and realized incremental–almost negligible–gains as a result. We believe that change requires a more radical path.

RADICAL INCLUSION IN THE TECHNOLOGY SECTOR

In 2019, Marlo conducted research benchmarking best practices for inclusion in four kinds of spaces that are central to high-growth-oriented tech founders: coworking spaces, accelerators, incubators, and conferences. It should be noted that some of the spaces observed were entrepreneurial hubs, which can combine several of these types of spaces. Coworking spaces, accelerators, incubators, and conferences can be permanent or temporary, depending on their structure and purpose. Her motivation for benchmarking was to add something to the conversation about inclusion in the world of technology entrepreneurship where I could focus on positive examples (Rencher, 2019).

Coworking spaces are typically permanent, physical, membership-based spaces. Their purpose is to provide a positive community for their members that helps to support their business goals. This is usually accomplished by the curated mix of members and programming provided in the space.

Accelerators are cohort-based, time-limited programs focused on helping companies to grow more rapidly than they would on their own. The mentors and networks affiliated with the accelerator are their primary source of differentiation. Accelerators with networks and mentors that can produce rapid growth have more applicants and are more competitive. Accelerators tend to have a specific industry or customer focus in order to filter applicants to tightly align with their existing mentors and networks. At the conclusion of each accelerator, there is a "Demo Day" where participants pitch their start-ups to investors on a stage in a highly choreographed PowerPoint-type presentation. These Demo Day pitches introduce the start-up and illustrate the growth that they have been able to achieve during the accelerator. Ultimately, the social capital garnered by being featured on stage is intended to translate into investment from angel investors and venture capitalists who could provide the funding they need to fuel more growth.

Incubators are more defined by space than time, in that they often occur in a specific physical setting for loosely defined periods of time, usually longer than the time an entrepreneur would participate in an accelerator. Start-ups in incubators are typically in their earliest stages, often before the idea has been proven. Their purpose is to provide support and guidance to nurture the start-up into being a viable business.

Conferences are gatherings with a particular theme or broad topic where participants learn and connect. They can last anywhere from a few hours to a week. Technology has become more integrated into the conference experience. Participants can be matched, tagged, and filtered for more efficient networking.

Methodology

The organizations Marlo selected to observe were distinguished by their focus on underrepresented technology entrepreneurs. In the context of this research, underrepresented technology-based entrepreneurs include women, Black, and Latinx founders. It also included people whose identities intersected more than one or even all of those categories.

Data was collected via participant observation, photos, and semi-structured interviews in three cities: Atlanta, Georgia; Memphis, Tennessee; and Miami, Florida. The Atlanta research was conducted in February 2019. The Miami research was conducted in April 2019. The Memphis research was conducted in June 2019. She visited coworking spaces, accelerators, incubators, and conferences supporting underrepresented technology-based entrepreneurs. The conferences drew participants from outside the local area. The accelerators and incubators tended to be established, persistent, inclusive spaces that drew a more local clientele.

Why is this relevant?

According to the United States Census Bureau's Business Dynamic Statistics, start-ups create about 43 percent of new jobs each year.

From 2000 to 2017, small businesses created 8.4 million net new jobs. Large corporations created 4.4 million net new jobs during the same time period. Imagine the economic impact if more of those new businesses—particularly those that produce high-wage, high-growth tech jobs—persisted beyond their first five years. According to CB Insights, 70 percent of start-up tech companies fail. Forty-two percent of these companies fail because there is not a market for the problem that they are trying to solve.

Tech entrepreneurship offers a powerful force when it comes to addressing both societal problems and opportunities. Generally speaking, underrepresented tech entrepreneurs are inadequately recruited, developed, and supported. Yet because companies run by underrepresented entrepreneurs are more likely to offer an inclusive culture, they offer a sustainable competitive advantage. Why? Because they can access new market opportunities unlocked by insight from underrepresented team members. People outside the dominant culture have a more clear-eyed vision of the dominant culture and of potential new/emergent markets. They can also solve problems with a different perspective. Companies with effectively managed diversified teams have also significantly better financial performance than those that lack diversity. According to the *Harvard Business Review*, diversity leads to innovation and higher revenue.

> *(C)ompanies with above-average total diversity, measured as the average of six dimensions of diversity (migration, industry, career path, gender, education, age), had both 19 percentage points higher innovation revenues and 9 percentage points higher EBIT margins, on average. All six dimensions of diversity had statistically significant correlations with innovation, both individually and collectively, although industry, nation of origin, and gender had slightly larger effects (Lorenzo & Reeves, 2018).*

Once underrepresented people are engaged, it is critically important that they are included in deep and meaningful ways. Working in a tech start-up—particularly in a leadership role—does not present the optimum environment for overall well-being. This is even more the case for underrepresented people at all levels of the organization.

> *"Given the extraordinary impact entrepreneurs have on our world economy, it's critically important they operate in a state of optimum emotional and relational health. Unfortunately, in our current zeitgeist of founder burnout as a benchmark of entrepreneurial excellence, such has not been the case."* (Muenster & Hokemeyer, 2019).

The research Marlo conducted investigates the best practices of organizations that effectively engage underrepresented people in tech entrepreneurship spaces such as incubators, accelerators, coworking spaces, and conferences. As a doctoral-level social scientist, she is intensely curious about this subject and clear about the potential for positive impact. The intent is to share these practices to help start-ups, entrepreneurial ecosystem partners, and government agencies to nurture inclusion, and ultimately belonging, in tech entrepreneurship.

Most tech companies lack diversity and inclusion. They have remained stubbornly monocultural, which prevents them from the competitive advantages that underrepresented groups provide. What follows is a clear, data-driven, and practical guide for engagement with underrepresented groups in tech spaces, which will help to combat the staggering rate of failure for these companies.

STRATEGIES FOR INCLUSION

The people leading the organizations and events employed several effective strategies and tactics that contributed to creating highly inclusive spaces. Below are five strategic categories with corresponding tactics that summarize the best practices observed.

Community Organizing

Community organizing is a powerful tool for engagement that shifts the focus from the individual to the collective, usually by appealing and affiliating all to a greater purpose. Corresponding activities include:

- Reinforce community through rituals and symbols— happy hours, meetups, food and drink

- Use "call-and-response" engagement. Call and response is a type of interaction where one party generates a verbal or written statement or embodied movement and calls for the intended audience to respond in kind.

Cultural Signifying

Marlo uses the phrase "cultural signifying" to indicate use of language, symbols, terms, and expressions that represent an authentic insider view are used. They allow people to:

- Reflect the culture in their community they serve through art and iconic representation

- Share ownership of space by asking people to mark it through expressing themselves via writing or drawing

Trauma-Informed Approach

Unacceptably, there are situations people come from where they were threatened and experienced psychological or even physical abuse. To counter this, inclusive organizations focused on:

- Maintaining psychological and physical safety

- Actively and passively communicating the presence of psychological and physical safety

- Recognizing that for underrepresented people, time not being "the other" is sacred time

The data supports this need for safety.

- Entrepreneurs are 5 percent more likely than the general public to report having a mental health condition

- And founders are:

  ‣ Twice as likely to suffer from depression

  ‣ Six times more likely to suffer from ADHD

  ‣ Three times more likely to suffer from substance abuse

  ‣ Ten times more likely to suffer from bipolar disorder

  ‣ Twice as likely to have psychiatric hospitalization

  ‣ Twice as likely to have suicidal thoughts

Relevant Representation

Kathryn Finney is the founder and former CEO of dig-italundivided, a pioneering organization that supports Black and Latinx women tech founders. As Ms. Finney says, "Tech is not looking for inclusion per se, but they're looking for assimilation. They're looking for Blacks and Latinos and women, but they are looking for these groups as versions of themselves."

Inclusive organizations ensure that the communities they serve see people who look like them at all levels of the organization, including senior leadership.

- They recognize the cost associated with not having inclusion as a part of the organization

- They find ways to build a strong and inclusive group identity to overcome imposter syndrome and isolation

Critical Race Theory

There is a demand to recognize that the uncompensated emotional, spiritual, and psychological labor placed upon underrepresented people to create safety for themselves may not be worth the effort for them.

Scholars such as Kimberlé Crenshaw and the late Harvard legal scholar Derrick Bell recognize the extent to which racism is woven into the structure of American society. The idea of racism as a permanent and unalterable feature of everyday life in the United States provides the context for how some underrepresented people navigate the tech entrepreneur space or go missing from it altogether.

Rather than try to achieve equality in access to resources and opportunities alternative strategies, frameworks, and models may be developed that ultimately lead to better outcomes.

As observed by Derrick Bell, "Success for the Black person requires effective functioning achieved with the knowledge that his or her work will not be recognized or rewarded to the same degree as a White person doing the same thing." He further notes that "Blacks must supplement the forms and patterns of striving for racial equality with innovative forms of personal self-image, group organization, resource collection and distribution, and strategic planning, using the concept of racial fortuity as a guideline."

STEPS TO IMPLEMENTATION OF FIVE STRATEGIES

The basic flow of the steps your organization must take to reach its next level is:

Step One: Assess current state

As previously discussed, you need to create a baseline of where your organization is right now in its diversity and inclusion efforts. If you don't have the training to do this, it is best to engage a qualified outside source.

Step Two: Create safety

In order to get an accurate picture of your organization and move forward toward your goals, you must create the conditions that enable your team to speak candidly, without fear of reprisal. The book *Crucial Conversations: Tools for Talking When Stakes Are High* by Al Switzler, Joseph Grenny, and Ron McMillan is an excellent primer on how to have conversations on subjects that are important but where opinions may vary. We will discuss how to use its framework in the next chapter.

Step Three: Communicate widely

Talk to as many people as possible about where you are now and what you see as weak areas. Feedback from people who left your organization, whether or not they are underrepresented, may be especially helpful.

Step Four: Prioritize implementation

Once you have assessed where you are and gathered additional information from your team, move forward with urgency and action.

Step Five: Drive accountability

Create quantified goals with deadlines and have a single person accountable for achieving them, though a large team can be responsible for the goals. There should be absolute clarity on whether or not the goals were achieved.

Through these steps, the forward progression of an inclusive and better workplace will begin to take form.

#REPRESENTATIONMATTERS

Representation doesn't just matter as you are engaging with underrepresented tech entrepreneurs; it matters in all contexts. For example, Twitter is a popular platform for Black social media users. Consider the following information from Esther Akinola, independent content strategist and influencer marketing consultant (Akinola, 2020).

- Black people across the globe are three times more likely to post daily on Twitter than any other demographic

- In 2018, the top three most-tweeted campaigns were #TakeAKnee, #BlackLivesMatter and #MeToo. All are Black-issue centered hashtags.

- While being only 12.5 percent of the US population, African Americans make up 25 percent of US Twitter users.

This trend has only increased as 2020 saw a spike in online activism and social and political commentary.

Twitter recognizes the power of its Black user base and has made a significant commitment towards representation among its employee ranks. Dalana Brand, vice president, People Experience and Head of Inclusion and Diversity shared the platform's ongoing commitment in its 2020 Inclusion and Diversity Report (Brand, 2020).

> *"We've set an ambitious goal for 2025 of having at least 25 percent of our overall US workforce be underrepresented minorities — at least 10 percent of which will be Black Tweeps. These numbers aren't nearly big enough, especially in technical and leadership roles, but they do show that Twitter strives to be a leader of our industry when it comes to representation of Black employees."*

Twitter has increased its overall representation of Black employees from 3.4 percent at the end of 2017 to 6.3 percent at the end of August 2020, nearly doubling its numbers. The social media giant is on track to achieve its goals. Twitter has done so by leaning into the uncomfortable but crucial conversations and by going for deep engagement.

Representation in tech can also be championed outside of traditional tech companies.

After completing her undergraduate degree, Marlin was an aspiring mortician. She was introduced to the field of technology by a friend and it changed the trajectory of her life. At the age of twenty-five, she learned to code in seven different languages, all courtesy of a thirteen-week corporate program. She emerged as a mainframe programmer. Many years later, Marlin founded Sisters Code with a goal to "Awaken the Mature Geek," by empowering women ages twenty-five to eighty-five to explore the field of technology.

Sisters Code has engaged thousands of women of every age, some of whom have gone on to pursue careers in technology and tech entrepreneurship. As a woman of color in tech who founded an organization to bridge the gender and racial gap in tech, Marlin continues to question and defy industry leaders' favorite claim that they can't find diverse talent.

THE OPPORTUNITY

A person who wishes to make a difference by using their influence and attention to become an advocate of change and its implementation is always going to be welcome in the pursuit of true diversity and inclusion. We can learn many things from this chapter's teachings:

- Through the story revealed through Peter Thiel's course at Stanford and Max Levchin's guest lecture, a company can often struggle with the diversity versus comfort of an organization. In the case of PayPal, it was a company mainly consisting of nerdy guys who were most comfortable around like-minded nerds. This left no room for inclusion. Today, the tech industry still struggles with a resistance to inclusion.

- Technology is a perfect field to bring underserved and minority workers to well-paying jobs with solid futures. Through initiatives taking place, people are able to dive into the important areas of concern and potential in the African-American community and create a vibrant new workplace culture that allows for safe expression of individuality, while also contributing to a team and a product or service's best possibilities.

CHAPTER SEVEN

HOW TO INNOVATE INCLUSION

The hard reset we are advocating requires a new level of thinking. We've discussed the context for inclusion and why it is important to organizational success. The urgency of this reset is clear. Let us now articulate a fresh approach to inclusion that goes beyond data gathering and basic management. To meet this moment, we must innovate.

Innovation as it applies to inclusion demands that we do things differently and extend ourselves and our team members beyond our individual and collective comfort zones. It means that you don't just recruit at different universities, you may recruit people without degrees. You may start to realize that the best talent is unlikely to come to your booth at a job fair, you may have to find them months before they are ready to move on from their current opportunity. Your most valuable insights may come from people who spend the most face-to face time with your customers, not your product managers. What got you to where you are now is unlikely to get you to the next level.

In this chapter, we will explore three essential pillars for innovative inclusion. We will then describe in detail how to execute in three focus areas that are vital to inclusion at any organization.

THREE ESSENTIAL PILLARS

The three essential pillars for innovative inclusion rely upon an approach that has been adopted by corporate innovation teams since the early 1900s. At that time, much of the research and development at corporations were handled by independent laboratories and internal research and development was rare (Teece, 1988). One hundred years later, the vast majority of innovation was done in-house. But the speed at which change was happening at the dawn of the twenty-first century created a pendulum swing back to relying on external collaborators, now including small, nimble firms and emergent start-ups. This was based on the recognition that there is infinitely more expertise and agility outside of most large organizations than inside.

Being clear about the value that external collaborators bring to an organization's inclusion efforts is required to embrace the three essential pillars for inclusive innovation. The pillars are as follows: 1) recognize and recruit disruptors, 2) create new relationships, and 3) decenter the organization and recenter the people.

Recognize and recruit disruptors

To make change that can make people uncomfortable (and all power shifts make people uncomfortable), you need to have people on your team that are disruptors. You need to be a disruptor. We don't mean someone who can walk into a room, turn over a table and leave. That's easy. We're talking about someone who can enter a room and get everyone in the room to see that they need to rearrange the furniture, and do it with urgency. A critical part of this skill is being able to connect radical ideas with a current need or strategic objective. Effective disruptors help to create an inclusive culture by tying efforts into organizational goals, not just on-off workshops. Inclusion is their superpower, because they often work with people in an organization who are underestimated or undervalued, people whose voices are rarely heard, in order to achieve their objectives.

We challenge you to work with people who challenge you. Those who demand disruptive change as a condition of working with you. They will be necessary allies. Have them help you to sharpen the skills you need to disrupt the status quo. We will talk about the specifics of some of those skills later in this chapter.

Create new relationships

Create new kinds of relationships externally. One out-of-the-box strategy for building an inclusive culture is via acqui-hire. An acqui-hire is a strategic acquisition of a company by another company, usually for the purpose of quickly and efficiently getting rare talent on your team. Usually this is done when a start-up has people with a specific technical skill or experience. We believe this could also be an effective way of introducing a diverse team to a company, particularly one that has a particularly poor track record of retaining diverse talent.

Rather than just hiring one or two people into an organization that does not have an inclusive internal culture, the idea would be to acquire the services of a whole team that has experience and a track record of working together. It would be important for the team to retain its own culture and autonomy within the acquiring company. In many ways, this is the opposite of inclusion. It is, in fact, segregation. However, if your culture is toxic to people who are not White males, it may be a gateway that ultimately leads to inclusion. With this strategy, there is less isolation for the group, increased chance of retention, and the potential for acculturation rather than assimilation. Some of the best parts of the acquired group's culture could improve the larger organization.

Another strategy is to create new kinds of relationships internally. Employee resource groups (ERGs) are ripe for a shift in the way they create and capture value from a corporation. We will discuss specifics later in the chapter. The data may also reveal internal departments that could be benchmarks for inclusion for the entire organization.

You can also create relationships with new people. A specific benefit that diversity and inclusion experts can add is their networks. You could find your next corporate board member from groups like The Links or professional organizations like the National Hispanic MBA Association if you are working with someone who is familiar with the groups and can forge a meaningful partnership with them on your behalf.

Decenter the organization, recenter the people

It is critical that you understand that your organization's interests and the team's interests may not automatically overlap. Inclusion champions people over the organization, which paradoxically builds a stronger organization. Create space for team members to indicate what they value and figure out how you can support it. Twitter's efforts to amplify voices in the social justice movement through strategically placed billboards not only galvanized its user base, it helped to more firmly connect the BlackBirds, its Black-led employee resource group, to the organization. The pride that some of its team members took in their role sent a signal that Twitter is an inclusive and positive place to work in a much more authentic and powerful way than anything coming directly from the company.

Personalize the journey. Normalize having conversations about what comes after employees' time with the company and figure out how working at your organization can get them there. Figure out where the pain points are and work to alleviate them. This could include shifting the allocation of benefits to include paying off a portion of an employee's student loan.

Pay attention to the community you are in. Recognize that if members of the community your organization is in are significantly underrepresented, that is problematic. You need to investigate the pathways to employment and advancement and see whether they are open to members of the community. To recruit underrepresented, in-demand professionals, you need to recruit after work. They are not as likely to be available during the day because they are likely to be currently employed. Marlin was part of a team that made a shift to recruiting from the daytime to after hours in order to recruit a higher level of talent.

The organization had to operate differently from what they were used to, but it yielded much better results.

With no warm introduction to more high-potential positions, less-recruited people will take a low-level position to get their feet in the door. As part of her work with more than one company, Marlin collected and analyzed the résumés of all of her organization's frontline workers. She learned that some workers in these lower-skilled-requirement jobs had MBAs, associate's degrees, and various other skills and training that were beyond basic. She started to advocate for increased paths to leadership and higher potential jobs for these workers. They are ultimately going to be able to bring much more value than if she maintained the status quo.

More inclusion in organizational decision-making produces higher quality results. In one instance, Marlin worked for a government agency and ran a team that was deliberating making changes to the city bus lines. At a certain point in the discussion, she began to ask herself who wasn't in the room. After polling her team, she found that no one in the room actually used local public transportation. She connected with someone in the organization who was able to provide that perspective. That team member's perspective created a better outcome.

It is also important to ensure that your community is represented in the governance of your organization, particularly if it serves the immediate community.

Marlin served as Chief Diversity Officer of a Fortune 500 company that was moving from the suburbs to an urban center with a majority Black population. She helped to diversify the publicly traded company's board of directors and, as a result, gave the company a more inclusive perspective as they transferred their workers and connected to the culture of the city.

These pillars for innovative inclusion provide immense value once fully implemented within an organization. But change does not happen by simply embracing strategy. It requires skillful action, monitoring, and maintenance. In the next section, we will explore three focus areas in which skillful action can be leveraged to reset inclusion within your organization.

THREE FOCUS AREAS

There are three focus areas that can truly make a difference as you are implementing your hard reset. They are: 1) how to present diversity and inclusion data, 2) how to reinvent employee resource groups, and 3) how to have uncomfortable conversations. We will now delve into the tactical aspects of these areas, with an emphasis on the basic implementation steps.

How to present diversity and inclusion data

Data is truth. It is one of the most valuable things there are in any function of any organization, and diversity and inclusion is no different. There are no emotions or feelings inherent to data, just in our interpretation of it and in the choices we make because of the data.

As an experienced and respected diversity and inclusion executive, Marlin is steeped in the importance of capturing Equal Employment Opportunity Commission (EEOC) data as a vital and indispensable tool. EEOC data essentially paints a demographic picture of a company's workforce, including gender, race, ethnicity, veteran status, and other related information. The data collected is objective fact reported by employees. How it is used and interpreted is more subjective. Telling the story of the data in a simple, visually compelling, and accurate way is a critical skill for today's diversity and inclusion professionals.

We use a straightforward approach to presenting diversity and inclusion data to people in organizations. Before presenting any information, we must ensure that there are robust systems in place to capture data. We cannot change what we haven't measured. If measurement is built into an organization's activity rather than collected as an afterthought, it will be more accurate and complete.

Once data collection systems are in place and activated, the first step is to understand the strategic objectives driving the organization. There must be a clear connection drawn between the diversity and inclusion information presented and those strategic objectives. For example, if a company is focused on cutting costs, we might show how a pattern of hiring and promotion that is viewed as unfair impacts employee retention and highlight the associated cost. If there is increased pressure to innovate new product and service development, we might analyze the level of diversity among product development staff to provide the basis for recommendations on how to tap into different backgrounds to increase innovation.

The second step is to analyze the data. Take a hard look and go beyond the surface story of the numbers. Don't stop with the fact that, for example, 92 percent of leadership of an organization is White and male while only 43 percent of the overall workforce fits that demographic. Look at the trends over time. Is there a particular department driving that dynamic? Which leaders have more diverse direct reports? How long does it usually take to get a promotion, by race. Who tends to stay and who typically leaves? You don't have to stop at quantitative information. Talking to a wide range of team members over time provides a great deal of qualitative data that can yield insight.

The third step is to construct an easy-to-follow story about the organization that is driven by the data. Again, the story should closely connect to the strategic objectives of the organization. Try to tell your story as a series of clear, digestible ideas. For example, one idea could be that your organization has been a place where it is difficult for Black women to thrive. The building blocks of your story will be charts, graphs, and headlines. You might show the relative promotion and retention rates of Black women over time in two or three slides. The headline or subhead of the slide you would present that information on would not just show the objective fact, it would include some interpretation. Your audience should be able to interpret your information in seconds.

The last step is to practice giving your presentation to a coworker in another department to ensure it is interpreted in the way you desired. This may not be possible if the data may not be shared across departments, but it is a great way to find out what questions are generated by your presentation. You can have your answers ready, even generating additional slides to provide back-up data in an appendix to your presentation.

Data can drive the efforts to assess and enhance inclusion. Yet it is the people that are within any organization who will feel the impact of those efforts. Next we will talk about ERGs, one of the earliest and most common structures created by companies as a means to foster inclusion and create a deeper sense of belonging.

How to reinvent ERGs

Employee resource groups (ERGs) are immensely valuable entities in that they help to create a structure for corporate inclusion that is led by the people in the groups that the company is trying to include. They can represent a wide variety of communities within a company that is connected through a particular identity, including LGBTQIA+, African-American, women, and parent employees.

ERGs started as internal organizations for those who were in the minority on their jobs to connect, support their fair treatment and ultimate advancement. They have also traditionally helped to recruit others who share the same identity as employees into the larger organization. The pandemic taught us that doing things in the same way is unsustainable. Like other aspects of the company, ERGs must also innovate.

ERGs that operate as more than a social club share a few common characteristics. They meet regularly, have clear mission statements, and have continuously monitored and updated goals and objectives that are tied to the bottom-line goals and objectives of the larger organization. They celebrate their diversity and the benefit it can bring to an organization.

Marlin connected with a Latinx ERG group that demonstrated their connection to the organizational bottom line perfectly. They learned that the company was outsourcing marketing literature translation services from English to Spanish. The ERG came together and shared why they should be a part of this process. Not only was it their native language, but they wanted to help. As a business, wouldn't you rather invest in your employees instead of hiring out work to outside groups?

Knowing that you have employees with more skills to offer you than you even realize, how can you leverage the knowledge? Use innovative thinking to tap these unused skills intelligently. Ensure that there is some compensation–monetary or otherwise–provided in exchange to recognize the extra value.

We have discussed the tactics of data and of ERGs. Now let's look at the tactics of change through conversation. Because we are dealing with inclusion, and we are working against our most basic tendencies to stick with our tribe, these conversations for change will almost always be uncomfortable.

How to have uncomfortable conversations

The framework for influence from the book *Crucial Conversations* is one of the best tools we have come across for starting to make the changes that are required in order to develop your commitment to inclusion and experience the benefits of a diverse workforce. Crucial conversations can open the door to big cultural change. They are the center of this plan.

The Influencer Model consists of three parts:

1. Use six sources of influence: How will you motivate and enable change?

2. Find vital behaviors: What few behaviors will lead to the greatest amount of change?

3. Clarify measurable results: What do you want to achieve?

The diagnosis goes from clarifying measurable results to finding vital behaviors to using six sources of influence. The influence begins with the six sources and goes to clarifying measurable results. When used properly, this shows the guidance, direction, and trajectory an organization has the potential to reach.

Each of these three components must be broken down, starting with clarifying measurable results. To do this, answer this question: What results do you want to achieve?

These results need to be SMART, which is:

- Specific

- Measurable

- Attainable

- Relevant

- Time-bound

After this, you are going to define what vital behaviors are associated with the measurable results. You will need to:

- Identify the crucial moments

- Support each crucial moment with a vital behavior

Next, you will go into the diagnosis for the situation. This is when you will identify the barriers that are currently keeping people from engaging in the vital behaviors. This is broken down into six question groups.

Number one is centered on personal motivation.

Number two focuses on personal ability.

Numbers three and four focus on social motivation and ability.

Number five pertains to the structural motivation.

Number six addresses the structural ability.

Now, let's get to the questions:

1. What might people find painful, frightening, boring, or uncomfortable about the vital behaviors?

2. What skill gaps get in the way of doing the vital behaviors (physical skills, knowledge, understanding, social skills)?

3. What social influence challenges are you up against?

4. How are you or others discouraging the vital behaviors? How are you or others enabling the wrong behaviors?

5. Are there costs and penalties for doing the vital behaviors? Are people rewarded for behaving badly??

6. What environmental factors could enable the wrong behaviors (consider space, cues, data, and tools)?

With this section complete, it is time for you to use your six sources of influence (Yes, you have this). In doing so, you will be able to identify strategies in each source for how you'll influence people to engage in the vital behaviors. There are also six key questions for this section.

Here are the questions:

1. Consider: Field trips? Just try it? Tell a meaningful story? Allow for choice?

2. How can you employ deliberate practice?

3. How can you lead the way?

4. Who are the opinion leaders in the organization? What do you want them to do?

5. Use rewards in moderation; link rewards to vital behaviors.

6. What environmental factors could enable the vital behaviors (consider space, data, cues, and tools)?

This activity will help you spur on individual growth and corporate unity. It is a catalyst for becoming mindful of what messages you send out, intentionally or unintentionally, in your organization.

The recommendation is to have everyone in your organization take part in this exercise, including frontline workers and executives. Rallying people to get on board or step away starts with leadership.

THE OPPORTUNITY

Ways of addressing the new normal in the workplace are being unveiled every day. We have the opportunity to maximize this swiftly changing environment to be inclusive. In this chapter, we discussed some of the tactics that connect the change we want to create to the practical actions required to bring about that change.

You have learned:

- The three essential pillars for inclusive innovation: 1) recognize and recruit disruptors, 2) create new relationships, and 3) decenter the organization and recenter the people

- The three focus areas that can truly make a difference as you are implementing your hard reset: 1) how to present diversity and inclusion data, 2) how to reinvent employee resource groups, and 3) how to have uncomfortable conversations

- The Influencer Model offers a solid blueprint for all employees to engage in and determine many things about their work environment, including:

  ‣ Their personal motivation and ability to use their sources of influence for change and to diagnose what problems exist

‣ How their social beliefs and interactions impact their ability to put their best practices to use and feel motivated to do so

‣ Ways in which the structure of an organization can reward positive change over negative choices

‣ Gaining a better understanding of how your environment can enhance or cripple your ability to make changes

CHAPTER EIGHT

HOW TO KEEP YOUR SANITY

We have come to the final chapter.

For you, it is probably the most important one. These words are powerful because they are centered around you and your well-being. When we say you, we really mean you, specifically.

We mean you, the person who has taken the journey of this book and, hopefully, taken it as a challenge.

We mean you, the warrior, the catalyst, the instigator, the disruptor, the troublemaker, the agitator for change.

We mean you, the pragmatist, the one who knows this road is as much a fiduciary necessity as "the right thing to do."

We mean you, the one who suffers through eye-rolls, passive aggressiveness, and outright rudeness as you stare down the mediocracy and make a stand for the importance of diversity, equity, and inclusion.

This work is not for the faint of heart. It is depleting work. Therefore, it is imperative that you practice extreme self-care. The way to keep your sanity is for you to take extremely good care of yourself.

For some, to see the words "extreme self-care" conjures feelings of discomfort. The very idea of centering your well-being as THE highest priority seems a bit much. For you to make others accommodate your self-care requirements may feel like the ultimate in self-centered, me-first assholery.

What we're asking you to do is to let it be that. Let yourself be selfish. Let yourself put yourself first. Create bulletproof boundaries and respect them as you would respect a sacred house of worship. More than that, make others respect your boundaries, too.

If you are looking for permission, we just gave it to you.

The reason that it is okay for you to create a practice of extreme self-care is not because you are making the world a better place. You may put everything you've got into your efforts and not make a dent in your culture or your organization. It just may not work in the long or the short run.

The reason that it is okay for you to create a practice of extreme self-care is because you said so. That's it.

So let's get started.

SETTING BOUNDARIES

We have established that you don't need an excuse to practice extreme self-care. However, it may be helpful for you to understand some of the benefits of doing so.

One important benefit is that self-care establishes boundaries that enable you to move with confidence and ease. You can work with clarity and focus. With strong boundaries, you are highly equipped to deal with the inevitable discomfort that accompanies challenging other people's comfort zones.

Have you ever been in a situation when someone does or says something that you recognize as a put-down, micro-aggression, or even an overt attack? We've been there, and there were times when we have been shocked into silence. We have had internal conversations where we debate whether we really heard what we heard or saw what we saw. Sometimes enough time has passed (and that time can sometimes be only a minute or two), so that we feel awkward addressing what happened. We have left such situations feeling angry, not just because of what was said or done, but because we didn't address it in a powerful way.

What we've found over time and experience is that when our self-care practice is robust, then our boundaries are clear and well-maintained. We are more prepared to defend them when someone tries to breach them. We are grounded in our responses because We know, deeply know, what is permissible, what is not, and why.

Marlo recalls a story related to this dynamic.

"I had a job in an area that was very conservative and where there were not many Black people. I remember being in a meeting when I introduced myself to a some-what older White woman who was a prominent member of the community. She complimented my locs and reached out and held a few of them for a moment. I continued with the meeting, but in the back of my mind, I was still processing her casual intimacy and the fact that I just felt like I had been petted like a dog.

I was used to being in an environment where such contact simply would not have happened and I had not prepared myself for that type of encounter. I got to know the woman over time. Looking back on the moment, I'm sure that her intention was not to make me feel uncomfortable, but her intentions do not matter. What matters is that a boundary was violated. We don't need to interpret others' intentions to inform our actions and reactions— that is what our boundaries are for. Let the boundaries that you have created be your guide. You don't have to have let anyone else know in advance about them. They will learn when you tell them."

As we give ourselves more space to practice self-care, we strengthen our boundaries. We give ourselves the space and permission to not just say when our boundaries have been violated, but to also let people know when they are coming close to them. We move toward being unequivocal about clearly stating our needs and requirements.

THE IMPORTANCE OF EXTREME SELF CARE

Empaths are highly sensitive individuals who have the ability to sense what people are thinking and feeling. Psychologists may use the term empath to describe a person that experiences a great deal of empathy, often to the point of taking on the pain of others at their own expense.

More often than not, people who are involved in the civil rights movement—including those who choose to work in the field of diversity, equity and inclusion—are empaths. They see the inequities, they spend time speaking with people about their real-life experiences of being passed up for positions, being stereotyped, dealing with microaggressions, and facing discrimination.

Marlin often talks about how when she started this work, her office was a revolving door for team members to speak through their reality of injustice. One employee called her "Dr. Phil," and it caught on. Marlin thought it was funny until she realized it was true. Instead of working during the day, she had become the team member counselor as it related to diversity, equity and inclusion. She completely upended the notion of work-life balance as she took on this extra, unpaid burden. She handled her day-to-day responsibilities after hours and on weekends in an effort to be the listening ear for team members during normal working hours.

This work will show up in your personal life. This work will bring you to tears and cause you to neglect yourself and those you love.

The year 2020 was marked not only by the COVID-19 pandemic, it was also the year of the televised killing of George Floyd, the racial reckoning, and all the mental exhaustion that came along with them. The very first week of 2021 brought with it a terrorist attack on the US Capitol that was fueled by White supremacy and enabled by White privilege. Self-care is no longer a buzzword; it's imperative for this work to continue.

Self-care is anything we intentionally do with our well-being in mind. It is activated when we give ourselves the same grace that we give to others. While there are many things we can do to assure self-care, the following are tried and true.

Activate your village

The village I'm speaking of is your peers or others who are bold enough to advocate for diversity, equity, and inclusion. Most of these people have either made this their life's work or are true believers in the movement.

Marlin has been involved in this work for over twenty years, therefore she has organically tapped into a network of peers who are also passionate about this work. They check in with one another and have accountability groups. They connect not to talk about the work but to encourage self care.

Before the pandemic, eight of the women in Marlin's village met up in a beautiful yet remote location to practice extreme self-care. The majority of these women are recognized as experts in this field of work, while others were just beginning the journey. They were intentional in inviting the younger generation as they recognized the importance of actually showing them the importance of self-care in action before they experienced burnout.

During the retreat, the women did not talk about their work; it was not allowed. Instead they disconnected from work, turned off their phones, and began a different kind of work, the work of restoration. This restorative work included meditation, journaling, spa treatments, financial planning, quiet time, and naps.

Although the work connected to your job is important, you and your health are the most important! You cannot advocate for others if you have lost yourself.

Reach out to your professional network

There will be a time when you want to or have to speak with others about this work. You will see things you can't unsee and hear things you can't unhear. This is the time to reach out to your professional network.

Early in her career, Marlin remembers an executive saying to her, "I don't believe we discriminate; we treat coloreds the same as everyone else." And no, this was not in the 1960s! Marlin remembers hearing another leader say that he has no issue promoting a woman as long as she has one child. The leader indicated that the problem comes along with baby #2 because the woman is not committed to working overtime.

These are times when you engage your network of diversity, equity and inclusion professionals. Not to gossip about the stories as that serves no one, but to make sure you are staying sane and choosing the right way to address the inappropriate comments, actions and most importantly, seeking out someone to help you to not internalize the foolishness.

Diversity, equity, and inclusion work is a matter of the head and heart. Activate your village to protect your mental and emotional health. You must not hesitate to connect with the people who are doing the work. Trust me, they have some of the same stories and experiences. You are not alone.

If you don't have a network, that's totally fine. There are professional groups on social networks like LinkedIn or diversity organizations that will provide the assistance you need.

Be honest about progress

You work hard. You believe that things will change and they don't. People of color are still underrepresented in areas of the company, receiving the lowest ratings, making the least, mostly on the front line and the list goes on. This can be very disheartening and it's easy to take it personally. It's easy to believe that you have not worked hard enough and that you are letting people down.

Your organization can draft statements of equality, donate money to Black Lives Matter, and even make a firm commitment to diversity goals. Even with good intentions the needle doesn't move. Listen, you are there to present the truth, the data does not lie and no one can explain it away - it is what it is.

Your job is to share what is, ask the questions, and even suggest the way forward. However, more often than most, you are not the CEO or decision maker. Sit with that for a moment. Share the data, try to let go of the outcome and know that you have done your job. As a matter of fact, be proud. You've done what you could.

Engage a coach or a therapist

It's sometimes easy to process the thought that you may need a therapist or coach as it relates to your personal life. The same is true when it comes to your professional life, especially when you work in the field of diversity, equity and inclusion. How do we ask people to show up as their whole selves when we are depleted mentally and physically merely from the work we do?

After the January 6th, 2021, insurrection and riot at the United States Capitol, Marlin spoke about how the outcome would have been different if the people that showed up that day looked like her. This was White privilege shouting out loud! Although she knew that racism existed, that day took a different toll on her and she had to seek out help.

Do not look at it as a weakness to seek out professional help. This work is a heavy lift and it's easy to quit. We need you, the movement cannot be stopped. Many employers have Employee Assistance Programs; do not overlook this benefit.

TAKING CARE OF YOUR TEAM

Once you are able to operate from a place of personal abundance and wellness, it is much easier to take care of others. In this section, we will explore caring for your team. We are not talking about back rubs in the break room. What we mean by taking care of your team is making sure they feel supported, valued, and respected.

As the COVID-19 pandemic reshaped the work world, some of the rules changed. The rules that changed were both written and unwritten, spoken and unspoken. Suddenly, working from home was a requirement for many workers. They actually started to use the virtual tools that had been there for years. It also became clear that there is certain work that requires people to be present, whether on the factory floor, in the grocery store, or in the restaurant.

The workers who stayed home watched their commutes shorten, their grocery bills increase, their fuel purchases decrease, and their work wardrobe become much more, shall we say, stretchy. The workers whose jobs require their presence still had to get to work and deal with the associated costs. People in both groups have the additional pressure of securing child and elder care, but those working from home can be in a better position to take care of their dependents themselves.

If you are working from home or working at a job site, it can be easy to forget about the dynamics of someone in the other group. Those working from a home with internet connectivity issues and an ailing parent have a certain set of challenges. Those working in a bar where customers refuse to correctly wear their masks and lash their frustrations out on the staff have another set of challenges.

What is most important is that someone in a company is thinking about the entire team. Do team members feel as if they belong? Are they feeling valued and respected? Does one group feel unfairly treated? Does everyone have what they need to be their best? As a leader in inclusion, these concerns are your concerns.

Some issues can be addressed with a simple shift. It can be about making sure that everyone in a company gets important company-wide communications. For those who work at a desk or computer, it can be easy to communicate via an email or instant message. If communicating with your frontline workers is an afterthought, they consistently find out about important information after the rest of the employees. This can make those team members feel like less of a priority.

Try doing something different. Marlin created a communication strategy at her organization where frontline workers received corporate information at the same time as everyone else. The previous practice had been for essential workers to hear about news after their shift, which meant that they were usually the last to know. The new practice promoted inclusion and respect because it allowed them to provide feedback at the same time that other voices were heard. This feedback resulted in important adjustments that incorporated the needs of those workers.

It's not just frontline workers that need consideration. There are people who are dealing with added stressors as they witness incidents such as the attack on the nation's Capitol by rioters touting the symbols of White supremacy. There are people who are confounded by the logistics and complexity of supporting their children in their virtual classrooms. Others are mourning the deaths of friends and family to coronavirus; others still who are having a tough time processing the separation imposed by quarantining.

It is important to create policies that support workers as they navigate through these issues, without having them have to completely disclose their situations. Make time off and opportunities for reflection and self-growth a part of the experience of working with your organization.

Forward-thinking organizations have instituted policies that include company-wide mental health days off, paid sabbaticals, flexible professional development, on-site child care, and paid life coaching. You can innovate your own solutions in collaboration with your team to determine what fits. These practices can be a shrewd investment in securing the best talent. Ultimately, you must make the case for the solution that will move your organization forward.

THE OPPORTUNITY

According to Lauren Blackwood of Kings College London, "Conversations which challenge racial dynamics and hierarchies are not yet normalized. But what is normalized is the often-unquestioned dominance of White people and White-run institutions."

This racially based hegemony is often accompanied by dominance of other aspects of American normative behavior. Challenging cultural norms around gender, sexual orientation, socioeconomic status, ability, and age is extremely exhausting work. In order for you to do the work effectively, you must practice extreme self-care.

Take care of yourself, first. With you in full health and at your best, you can create boundaries that help you to maintain your sanity and your productivity. You can honor your empathic nature with intention by following these simple practices.

- Activate your village. Connect to your personal circle of friends to heal and restore.

- Reach out to your professional network. Share best practices and grow better, together.

- Be honest about progress. Be clear how far your company is moving the needle. If they are being insincere and ineffective despite your best efforts, it may be time to move on.

- Engage a coach or therapist. The top professionals in the world have professional help, whether it is sports, politics, or business. You should not hesitate to do the same.

As you elevate yourself, you will inspire others. Make sure you go beyond inspiration to help create policy to take care of your team. Ask all the members of your team what their concerns are and find innovative ways to help bring their best selves to the job.

CONCLUSION

THE CROSSROADS

We are at a crossroads, friends. Now it is up to us to bridge the divide and open the gates to creating strong, effective, and fruitful diversity, equity, and inclusion in the workplace. Will it be easy? Probably not. When you change a culture you also need to shift the mindsets of those people in it. This is the entire purpose of what we have shared with you. There are a few thoughts we would like to leave with you.

- Face the uncomfortable truths that have worked against the progress of initiatives that bridge the gap between essential and nonessential workers, particularly during the COVID-19 pandemic.

- Data has become more accessible than ever, and with that comes the use of cell phones and a desire to record everything. With this potential, businesses are at risk of being exposed for non-inclusive practices.

- There is no longer an acceptable excuse for knowing what should be done for diversity, equity and inclusion, including how employees work with COVID-19, and not taking action to resolve the inequities in the workplace.

- Through data, we can paint the real story of where a business is with its diversity. Most fall short of hopes and expectations, which means they have work to do.

- To start change, it is important to assess where your business stands currently. Through the content in this book, you can gauge where your business aligns compared with others.

- The good, the bad, and the ugly—COVID-19 revealed them all in one way or another. These case studies help us learn how we can grow, improve, and start to thrive more abundantly.

- All organizations can develop the skills and tools it takes to be advocates of initiatives that protect all workers and create an inclusive culture.

- We are required to take care of ourselves both personally and professionally in order to be the best we can be at work and in our lives outside of the workplace

We don't need everyone to agree with everything we said in this book for this book to make a difference. We need them to be vested in the vision of stronger and better businesses through the equitable representation and the opportunities that come when everyone is given a chance at success.

Real, meaningful, lasting change takes skill, work, and a little faith. Your opportunity starts now, whether you are just embarking on your journey or you feel as if you have been advocating for change your entire life. Know that we are here to cheer you on, to lift you up, to add our collective expertise to your own, and to celebrate your wins. You are not alone.

Marlo and Marlin

www.hardresetinclusion.com

ABOUT THE AUTHORS

MEET MARLO RENCHER

Dr. Marlo Rencher is an entrepreneur, anthropologist and educator with over two decades of experience in start-up and small business development. She is a cofounder at Commune Angels, an inclusive network of angel investors. She is the founder of Tech Founders Academy, which helps Black and Brown women reinvent themselves as Tech Founders. She has also founded or cofounded three other tech start-ups.

Marlo was the coauthor of digitalundivided's 2016 #ProjectDiane report, which provided groundbreaking insight into the funding gap for Black women tech founders. Her research on developing inclusive tech accelerators, incubators, coworking spaces, and entrepreneurial hubs continues to impact over one hundred founders each year who participate in programs informed by the research findings.

Marlo earned an undergraduate degree in marketing from Michigan State University, an MBA from the Ross School of Business at the University of Michigan, and a PhD in business and organizational anthropology from

Wayne State University. She earned the Certified Diversity Executive credential through the Institute for Diversity Certification. Marlo frequently speaks on technology entrepreneurship and inclusion and has been a presenter at TEDxDetroit, Princeton University, and SXSW.

MEET MARLIN WILLIAMS

Marlin G. Williams has over twenty years' experience as a global diversity and inclusion officer for two Fortune 500 organizations. She is an international speaker, media contributor, former deputy chief information officer and technology entrepreneur.

Marlin began her career as an aspiring mortician until she fell into the world of technology while attending a program at Compuware Corp. There she learned to program in seven different languages in thirteen weeks and emerged as a mainframe programmer, which changed the trajectory of her life. Marlin went on to create and implement the organization's award-winning diversity, equity and inclusion strategy, which tremendously increased the number of women and people of color in tech.

Marlin was selected to serve as the city of Detroit's deputy CIO. During her tenure, she and her team successfully developed the city's first e-government initiative and led collaboration across ten agencies to support the technology and infrastructure for Super Bowl XL.

Marlin was the inaugural diversity and inclusion entrepreneur-in-residence at a major economic development organization. She focused on bridging the racial and gender gap in tech entrepreneurship. Marlin built the first suite of inclusive tech entrepreneurship programs that ran from ideation to funding, which successfully increased the number of racially and gender diverse tech founders.

Marlin is also the founder of Sisters Code, which is on a mission to "Awaken the Mature Geek" by empowering women ages twenty-five to eighty-five to explore the world of coding and technology. Sisters Code has taught thousands of women the skills needed to become developers.

Marlin earned an undergraduate degree from Wayne State University, a master's degree from University of Detroit Mercy, certification in organizational development with an emphasis in diversity and inclusion from DePaul University and certification in employee relations law from the Institute of Applied Management. Marlin is also a certified life coach and the host of the *My Peace is Non-Negotiable* podcast, in which she empowers women to live the life they never thought possible.

Marlin frequently speaks on topics related to diversity, equity and inclusion, tech inclusion, entrepreneurship, and women's empowerment. She has delivered insightful and thought-provoking presentations to Microsoft, TEDx, SXSW, Techonomy, MSNBC, NBC, Techweek, Twitter, LinkedIn, Google, and others.

APPENDIX A: GLOSSARY

IDENTITIES

Our identities are who we are as individuals, including our personal characteristics, history, personality, name, and other attributes that make us unique and different from other individuals.

ADOS: American Descendants of Slavery. A term started by Yvette Carnell and Antonio Moore that seeks to provide context for African American identity and experience that is grounded in its unique lineage and connected to their continuing struggle for social and economic justice in the United States.

Asexual: someone who does not experience sexual attraction.

Bigender/Dual Gender: a person who possesses and expresses a distinctly masculine persona and a distinctly feminine persona and is comfortable in and enjoys presenting in both gender roles.

BIPOC: Black Indigenous People of Color. This term is intended to help capture the distinction (that usually bears out in differences in treatment) between people of color, Black people, and Indigenous communities. BIPOC is pronounced "buy pock" ("pock" as in "pocket"). You don't pronounce each letter separately, so you wouldn't say "B-I-P-O-C."

Biracial: a person who identifies as coming from two races; a person whose biological parents are of two different races.

Bisexual: a person who is attracted to people of their own gender as well as another gender.

Cisgender: a description for a person whose gender identity, gender expression and sex assigned at birth align (e.g., man, masculine, and male).

Ethnicity: the culture of people in a given geographic region, including their language, heritage, religion, and customs.

First Nations People: individuals who identify as those who were the first people to live on the Western Hemisphere continent; people also identified as Native Americans.

Gender: social, cultural, and psychological traits linked to females and males that define them as feminine or masculine.

Gender Identity: refers to a person's internal, deeply felt sense of being a man or woman, or something other or in between, which may or may not correspond with the sex assigned at birth; because gender identity is internal and personally defined, it is not visible to others.

Heterosexual: a person attracted to members of another sex or gender.

Homosexual: a person who is attracted to members of what they identify as their own sex or gender (the terms Gay and Lesbian are preferred).

Intersex: a general term used for a variety of conditions in which a person is born with reproductive organs, sexual anatomy or chromosomes that are not considered "standard" for either male or female.

LGBTQIA: an inclusive term for those who identify as lesbian, gay, bisexual, transgender, queer or questioning, intersex and asexual.

Multiracial: a person who identifies as coming from two or more races; a person whose biological parents are of two or more different races.

Multiethnic: a person who identifies as coming from two or more ethnicities; a person whose biological parents are of two or more ethnicities.

Pansexual (also referred to as omnisexual or polysexual): referring to the potential for sexual attractions or romantic love toward people of all gender identities and biological sexes; the concept of pansexuality deliberately rejects the gender binary.

People of Color: used primarily in the United States to describe any person who is not White; the term is meant to be inclusive among non-White groups, emphasizing common experiences of racism.

Queer: an umbrella term that can refer to anyone who transgresses society's view of gender, sexual orientation, or sexuality.

Questioning: refers to an individual who is uncertain of her/his sexual orientation, gender, or identity.

Race: refers to the concept of dividing people into populations or groups on the basis of various sets of physical characteristics that result from genetic ancestry. Sociologists use the concept of race to describe how people think of and treat groups of people, as people very commonly classify each other according to race (e.g., as African American, or as Asian). Most sociologists believe that race is not "real" in the sense that there are no distinctive genetic or physical characteristics that truly distinguish one group of people from another; instead, different groups share overlapping characteristics.

Religion: a system of beliefs, usually spiritual in nature, and often in terms of a formal, organized denomination.

Sex: separate from gender, this term refers to the cluster of biological, chromosomal, and anatomical features associated with maleness and femaleness in the human body. Sexual dimorphism is often thought to be a concrete reality, whereas in reality the existence of intersex individuals points to a multiplicity of sexes in the human population. Sex is often used synonymously with gender in this culture. Although the two terms are related, they should be defined separately to differentiate the biological ("sex") from the sociocultural ("gender").

Sexual Orientation: refers to the gender(s) that a person is emotionally, physically, romantically, and erotically attracted to. Examples of sexual orientation include homosexual, bisexual, heterosexual and asexual. Trans and gender-variant people may identify with any sexual orientation, and their sexual orientation may or may not change before, during or after gender transition.

Social Identity: involves the ways in which one characterizes oneself, the affinities one has with other people, the ways one has learned to behave in stereotyped social settings, the things one values in oneself and in the world, and the norms that one recognizes or accepts governing everyday behavior.

Transgender: has many definitions. It is frequently used as an umbrella term to refer to all people who deviate from their assigned gender at birth or the binary gender system. This includes transsexuals, cross-dressers, genderqueers, drag kings, drag queens, two-spirit people, and others. Some transgender people feel they exist not within one of the two standard gender categories but rather somewhere between, beyond or outside of those two genders.

Transsexual: refers to a person who experiences a mismatch of the sex he/she was born as and the sex he/she identifies as. A transsexual sometimes undergoes medical treatment to change his/her physical sex to match his/her sex identity through hormone treatments and/or surgically. Not all transsexuals can have or desire surgery.

TYPES OF BIAS

Bias is prejudice in favor of or against one thing or group compared with another, usually in a way considered to be unfair.

Ableism: prejudiced thoughts and discriminatory actions based on differences in physical, mental, and/or emotional ability; usually that of able-bodied/minded persons against people with illness, disabilities, or less developed skills.

Anti-Semitism: the fear or hatred of Jews, Judaism, and related symbols.

Biphobia: the fear or hatred of persons perceived to be bisexual.

Classism: prejudiced thoughts and discriminatory actions based on difference in socio-economic status, income, class; usually by upper classes against lower classes.

Discrimination: actions based on conscious or unconscious prejudice that favor one group over others in the provision of goods, services, or opportunities.

Hate Crime: Hate-crime legislation often defines a hate crime as a crime motivated by the actual or perceived race, color, religion, national origin, ethnicity, gender, disability, or sexual orientation of any person.

Heterosexism: viewing the world only in heterosexual terms, thus denigrating other sexual orientations.

Homophobia: the fear or hatred of homosexuality (and other nonheterosexual identities) and persons perceived to be gay or lesbian.

Implicit Bias: occurs when someone consciously rejects stereotypes and supports antidiscrimination efforts but also holds negative associations in his/her mind unconsciously.

In-group Bias: the tendency for groups to "favor" themselves by rewarding group members economically, socially, psychologically, and emotionally in order to uplift one group over another.

Islamaphobia: the fear or hatred of Muslims, Islam, and related symbols.

Marginalized: excluded, ignored, or relegated to the outer edge of a group/society/community.

Microaggression: everyday insults, indignities and demeaning messages sent to historically marginalized groups by well-intentioned members of the majority group who are unaware of the hidden messages being sent.

Misogynoir: a term coined by Moya Bailey and developed to describe the specific hatred, dislike, distrust, and prejudice directed toward Black women.

Misogyny: hatred of, aversion to, or prejudice against women

Oppression: results from the use of institutional power and privilege where one person or group benefits at the expense of another; oppression is the use of power and the effects of domination.

Prejudice: a preconceived judgment about a person or group of people, usually indicating negative bias.

Racism: prejudiced thoughts, discriminatory actions, *and systemic oppression* based on difference in race/ethnicity, usually by White/European descent groups against people of color.

Sexism: prejudiced thoughts and discriminatory actions based on difference in sex/gender, usually by men against women.

Silencing: the conscious or unconscious processes by which the voice or participation of particular social identities is excluded or inhibited.

Stereotype: blanket beliefs, unconscious associations, and expectations about members of certain groups that present an oversimplified opinion, prejudiced attitude, or uncritical judgment. Stereotypes go beyond necessary and useful categorizations and generalizations in that they are typically negative, are based on little information and are highly generalized.

System of Oppression: conscious and unconscious, nonrandom, and organized harassment, discrimination, exploitation, prejudice, and other forms of unequal treatment that impact different groups.

Transphobia: the fear or hatred of persons perceived to be transgender and/or transsexual.

Xenophobia: the fear or hatred of foreigners.

OTHER HELPFUL TERMS

Advocate: someone who speaks up for her/himself and members of his/her identity group, e.g., a woman who lobbies for equal pay for women. Advocates acknowledge responsibility as citizens to shape public policy to address intentional or unintentional harm to minorities and the oppressed, whether caused by action or inaction.

Ally: someone who speaks on behalf of others in need or distress until they are empowered to speak for themselves.

Bias Incident: a discriminatory or hurtful act that appears to be motivated or is perceived by the victim to be motivated all or in part by race, ethnicity, color, religion, age, national origin, sex, disability, gender identity, or sexual orientation. To be considered an incident, the act is not required to be a crime under any federal, state, or local statutes.

Color Blind: the belief in treating everyone "equally" by treating everyone the same; based on the presumption that differences are, by definition, bad or problematic and therefore best ignored (i.e., "I don't see race, gender, etc.").

Dialogue: "communication that creates and recreates multiple understandings" (Wink, 1997); it is bidirectional, not zero-sum and may or may not end in agreement. Dialogue can be emotional and uncomfortable, but is safe, respectful and has greater understanding as its goal.

Diversity: the representation of varied identities and differences (race, ethnicity, gender, disability, sexual orientation, gender identity, national origin, tribe, caste, socio-economic status, thinking and communication styles, etc.), collectively and as individuals.

Doing Gender: the notion that gender emerges not as an individual attribute but as something that is accomplished in interaction with others.

Dominant Culture: the cultural values, beliefs and practices that are assumed to be the norm and are most influential within a given society.

Equity: fair treatment, equality of opportunity, and fairness in access to information and resources for all.

Inclusion: the creation of a culture of belonging by actively inviting the contribution and participation of all people.

Privilege: a right, license or exemption from duty or liability granted as a special benefit, advantage, or favor.

Safe Space: refers to an environment in which everyone feels comfortable expressing themselves and participating fully without fear of attack, ridicule, or denial of experience.

Social Justice: is both a process and a goal. The goal of social justice is full and equal participation of all groups in a society that is mutually shaped to meet their needs. Social justice includes a vision of society in which the distribution of resources is equitable and all members are physically and psychologically safe and secure.

Tolerance: acceptance and open mindedness to different practices, attitudes, and cultures; does not necessarily connote agreement with the differences.

This glossary was compiled from existing resources provided by the National Conference for Community and Justice, Oregon State University, Arizona State University, Intergroup Relations Center, *Gender Roles: A Sociological Perspective, 5/e* by Linda Lindsey. Pearson/Prentice-Hall, 2011, The National Center for Transgender Equality, gaycenter.org, and chegg.com, Gender Equity Resource Center, BGSU, University of Michigan, Indiana University, Teaching for Diversity and Social Justice (Ed by Maurianne Adams, Lee Anne Bell, Pat Griffin).

ADDITIONAL SOURCES

Washington University in St. Louis:
https://diversityinclusion.wustl.edu/brss/glossary-of-bias-terms

Ford Foundation:
https://www.fordfoundation.org/about/people/diversity-equity-and-inclusion

REFERENCES

CHAPTER ONE: ON BELONGING

Developing Sensitivity to the Struggle

Barber II, W. J., & Kennedy III, J. (2020, April 27). Opinion: The pandemic changed our definition of 'essential.' Will we act on what we learned? Washington Post. https://www.washingtonpost.com/opinions/2020/04/27/pandemic-changed-our-definition-essential-will-we-act-what-we-learned/

Capehart, J. (2020, April 28). Coronavirus is exploiting 'the fissures of society,' the Rev. William Barber says. Washington Post. https://www.washingtonpost.com/opinions/2020/04/28/coronavirus-is-exploiting-fissures-society-rev-william-barber-says/

Coleman-Jensen, A., Rabbitt, M. P., Gregory, C. A., & Singh, A. (2020). Household Food Security in the United States in 2019 (ERR-275). U.S. Department of Agriculture, Economic Research Service.

Feeding America. (2020, October). The Impact of the Coronavirus on Food Insecurity in 2020. https://www.feedingamerica.org/sites/default/files/2020-10/Brief_Local%20Impact_10.2020_0.pdf

CHAPTER TWO: ON UNCOMFORTABLE TRUTHS

COVID-19: A Call for Change

Lithwick, D. (2020, April 21). America's Heroism Trap. Slate Magazine. https://slate.com/news-and-politics/2020/04/coronavirus-humans-vs-heroes.html

O'Reilly, A. (2020, April 20). Michigan Governor Whitmer sets up coronavirus racial disparity task force. Fox News. https://www.foxnews.com/politics/michigan-governor-whitmer-sets-up-coronavirus-racial-disparity-task-force

Cutter, C., & Maloney, J. (2020, March 22). With Business Turned Upside Down, CEOs Face Monumental Leadership Challenge. WSJ. https://www.wsj.com/articles/with-business-turned-upside-down-ceos-face-monumental-leadership-challenge-11584891047

Comfortable Lies

Serwer, A. (2020, June 16). America's Racial Contract Is Showing. The Atlantic. https://www.theatlantic.com/ideas/archive/2020/05/americas-racial-contract-showing/611389/

Are You Racist?

Waldman, K. (2018, July 23). A Sociologist Examines the "White Fragility" That Prevents White Americans from Confronting Racism. The New Yorker. https://www.

newyorker.com/books/page-turner/a-sociologist-examines-the-white-fragility-that-prevents-white-americans-from-confronting-racism

The Friction Points Within Organizations

Wirfs-Brock, J., & Paterson, L. (2017, June 15). IE Questions: What Is Inertia? And What's Its Role In Grid Reliability? Inside Energy. http://insideenergy.org/2015/06/15/ie-questions-what-is-inertia-and-whats-its-role-in-reliability/

Introspection

Morukian, M. (2020, May 4). Expansion: The Missing Link To Sustainable Diversity And Inclusion. Forbes. https://www.forbes.com/sites/ellevate/2020/05/04/expansion-the-missing-link-to-sustainable-diversity-and-inclusion/#58ddd28c1985

CHAPTER THREE: ON DATA DRIVEN DIVERSITY AND INCLUSION

Whalen, A. (2019, August 27). The True Story of the Flamin' Hot Cheetos Inventor Richard Montañez. Newsweek. https://www.newsweek.com/flamin-hot-cheeto-movie-true-story-creator-richard-montanez-1456377

City of Chicago. (2020, April 6). Mayor Lightfoot and CDPH Release New Demographic Data Release to

COVID-19 Revealing Significant Racial Health Inequities. Chicago.Gov. https://www.chicago.gov/city/en/depts/mayor/press_room/press_releases/2020/april/COVID19RacialInequities.html

Employee Loyalty in the Age of the Free Agent

Smothers, H. (2017, August 14). The Raw, Amazing Story of How Bozoma "Badass Boz" Saint John Became the CBO of Uber. Cosmopolitan. https://www.cosmopolitan.com/career/a10377753/bozoma-saint-john-uber-get-that-life/

Indicators for Inclusion

First Round Review. (n.d.). Here's How to Wield Empathy and Data to Build an Inclusive Team. https://review.firstround.com/heres-how-to-wield-empathy-and-data-to-build-an-inclusive-team

The Details are in the Dashboard

Intuit D&I Dashboard: https://www.ceoaction.com/media/2521/intuit-di-dashboard.jpg

Cambridge, MA Dashboard: https://www.cambridgema.gov/departments/equityandinclusion/interactiveequityandinclusiondashboard

CHAPTER FOUR: ON THE INCLUSION IMPERATIVE

Affirmative Action and Diversity: History and Key Distinctions

CNN Editorial Research. (2020, November 15). Affirmative Action Fast Facts. CNN. https://edition.cnn.com/2013/11/12/us/affirmative-action-fast-facts/index.html

Johnston, W. B., & Packer, A. E. (1987, January). Workforce 2000: Work and Workers for the 21st Century. Hudson Institute. https://files.eric.ed.gov/fulltext/ED290887.pdf

The Post-Pandemic Emergence of Inclusion Initiatives

Elias, J. (2020, September 29). Google's $310 million sexual harassment settlement aims to set new industry standards. CNBC. https://www.cnbc.com/2020/09/29/googles-310-million-sexual-misconduct-settlement-details.html

Glaser, A. (2020, May 19). Current and ex-employees allege Google drastically rolled back diversity and inclusion programs. NBC News. https://www.nbcnews.com/news/us-news/current-ex-employees-allege-google-drastically-rolled-back-diversity-inclusion-n1206181

Times of Crisis

Weise, K., & Conger, K. (2020, April 6). Gaps in Amazon's Coronavirus Response Fuel Warehouse Workers' Demands. The New York Times. https://www.nytimes.com/2020/04/05/technology/coronavirus-amazon-workers.html

Sacks, B. (2020, April 18). Costco Is Thriving During The Coronavirus Pandemic. Its Employees Have Paid The Price. BuzzFeed News. https://www.buzzfeednews.com/article/briannasacks/costco-thriving-coronavirus-pandemic-workers-pay

Samaha, A. (2020, March 28). Coronavirus: Starbucks Employees Got Sick. Stores Stayed Open. BuzzFeed News. https://www.buzzfeednews.com/article/albertsamaha/coronavirus-starbucks-stores-open-retail-employees-scared

Zhong, R. (2020, March 18). The Coronavirus Exposes Education's Digital Divide. The New York Times. https://www.nytimes.com/2020/03/17/technology/china-schools-coronavirus.html

Reston, M. C. (2020, April 9). Pandemic underscores digital divide facing students and educators - CNNPolitics. CNN.https://edition.cnn.com/2020/04/09/politics/digital-divide-education-coronavirus/index.html

PRISM International. (2013). Case Study: Verizon Wireless and Developing Women Leaders. http://www.prismdiversity.com/downloads/VZW_WomenLeaders.pdf

Tapia, A. (2019, May 28). Case Study: Diversity and Inclusion Transformation at Barilla SHRM Executive Network Blog. https://blog.shrm.org/executive/blogpost/case-study-diversity-and-inclusion-transformation-at-barilla/?_ga=2.264903110.85518757.1614210025761730245.1614210025

Case Studies - Companies that are changing the equation with Diversity and Inclusion. (2019, April 12). Andragogy Enabling Possibilities. https://www.shradhahrd.com/blog/case-studies-companies-changing-equation-diversity-inclusion/

Ganguli, S., & Murphy, G. (2019, April 12). Building Inclusion from the Inside-Out: A Brief Case Study (SSIR). Stanford Social Innovation Review. https://ssir.org/articles/entry/building_inclusion_from_the_inside_out_a_brief_case_study

Blueprints for Change

Emond, L., & Maese, E. (2021, January 29). Evolving COVID-19 Responses of World's Largest Companies. Gallup.Com. https://www.gallup.com/workplace/308210/evolving-covid-responses-world-largest-companies.aspx

Bersin, J. (2020, October 8). COVID-19 May Be The Best Thing That Ever Happened To Employee Engagement. JoshBersin.Com. https://joshbersin.com/2020/04/covid-19-may-be-the-best-thing-that-ever-happened-to-employee-engagement/

CHAPTER SIX: HOW TO MAKE CHANGE

Loder, C. [@chadloder]. (2019, October 19). Lack of diversity in tech is no accident. Peter Thiel, founder of PayPal, returned to his alma mater Stanford [Tweet]. Twitter. https://twitter.com/chadloder/status/1185634274529009

Reporting the Results

Umoh, R. (2020, May 7). Google Diversity Report Shows Little Progress For Women And People Of Color. Forbes. https://www.forbes.com/sites/ruthumoh/2020/05/05/google-diversity-report-shows-little-progress-for-women-and-people-of-color/#3c687af0207f

Radical Inclusion in the Technology Sector

Rencher, M. (2019, December). Radical Inclusion in Tech. TechTown Detroit. https://techtowndetroit.org/radicalinclusionintech/

Lorenzo, R., & Reeves, M. (2020, September 16). How and Where Diversity Drives Financial Performance. Harvard Business Review. https://hbr.org/2018/01/how-and-where-diversity-drives-financial-performance

Muenster, M., & Hokemeyer, P. (2019, March 22). There is a mental health crisis in entrepreneurship. Here's how to tackle it. World Economic Forum. https://www. weforum.org/agenda/2019/03/how-to-tackle-the-mental-health-crisis-in-entrepreneurship/

#RepresentationMatters

Akinola, E. (2020, February 21). Why Black Twitter matters for brands. PR Week. https://www.prweek.com/article/1674744/why-black-twitter-matters-brands

Brand, D. (2020, December). Inclusion & Diversity Q4 2020: Leadership, transparency & accountability. Twitter. https://blog.twitter.com/en_us/topics/company/2020/inclusion-and-diversity-report-q4-2020-leadership-transparency-and-accountability.html

CHAPTER SEVEN: HOW TO INNOVATE INCLUSION

Three Essential Pillars

Teece, D. J. (1988). Technological change and the nature of the firm. In G. Dosi, C. Freeman, R. Nelson, G. Silverberg, & L. Soete (Eds.), Technical Change and Economic Theory (pp. 256–281). Pinter Publishers.

Made in the USA
Monee, IL
23 June 2021